SOCCER'S STRANGEST MATCHES

Soccer's Strangest Matches

Andrew Ward

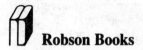 **Robson Books**

First published in Great Britain in 1989 by Robson Books Ltd, Bolsover House, 5–6 Clipstone Street, London W1P 7EB.

This Robson paperback edition first published 1992.

British Library Cataloguing in Publication Data
Ward, Andrew, 1949 –
  Soccer's Strangest Matches
  1. Association football matches to 1989
  I. Title
  796.334'09

ISBN 0 86051 600 8 (hb)
     0 86051 771 3 (pbk)

Printed in Great Britain by
Biddles Ltd, Guildford and Kings Lynn

Contents

Introduction

In the beginning they were all strange games. When the first official club — Sheffield, in 1857 — was formed, there were no other teams to play against. So the bachelors played the married men — until a nearby garrison put up a challenge. And one early Sheffield rule stipulated that players must hold half-crown coins while they played — to prevent pushing with the open hand.

In compiling this book I have tried to avoid such weird evolutionary encounters, opting instead for games played under more formal rules as we know them. Selected from over 110 years of soccer history, each game is strange, providing some new experience either for spectators or players. Sometimes people went to a game expecting novelty, as happened with the hypnotist at Hinckley or the New Bedford men against the Preston women. On other occasions one person has made a sensational impact on the game, whether through failure (like Jimmy Warner of Aston Villa), success (like Wilfred Minter of St Albans City) or a perverse mixture of both (like Chris Nicholl of Aston Villa). But the most obvious candidates for inclusion are those games in which events have simply departed from football tradition and entered a new world, beyond the control of the participants. Who could anticipate a dog heading a goal or a referee scoring the winning goal of a Football League match? Other matches derive their strangeness from tragedy. I have felt it necessary to include reminders of this, such as the impact of lightning at Aldershot in 1948, but I have deliberately omitted crowd disasters as I am completing the book in the aftermath of the 1989 Hillsborough disaster.

Strangeness, of course, is relative and culturally rooted. Inevitably, this collection is a personal selection. It draws heavily on the British professional scene, the section of soccer history with which I am most familiar, and only occasionally crosses national boundaries. I suspect that there have been even stranger matches around the world, or in the local leagues, well deserving of mention. For instance, I have heard of a player scoring the winning goal without coming on the field; apparently, as a substitute, he immediately took a corner-kick and fell over with a broken ankle as the ball curled into the net. And an editor friend, Graham Hart, once asked me how a player could score three goals without any other player touching the ball. The answer, in case you haven't worked it out, is that he scores an own-goal, picks the ball out of the net, carries it to the halfway-line, kicks off by angrily hoofing the ball high in the air and runs after it full-pelt. He is just inside the penalty area when he is tripped, whereupon he grabs the ball (still not touched by anybody), puts it on the penalty spot, slams it into the net and runs, Eusebio-like, to collect it himself. The referee blows for half-time, so the player hangs on to the ball and his team has the kick-off. Once more he punts the ball high in the air and, lo and behold, he is tripped again and scores from another penalty, his third goal without anyone touching the ball.

To the best of my knowledge that has never happened in a game. If it has, or you can think of any games that I have omitted, please drop me a line at Robson Books.

With this volume I have relied on others to point me towards a few of the games. Earlier versions of three of these stories appeared in *The Footballer* magazine. My sincere thanks to Anton Rippon, Ian Alister, John Harding,

Soccer's Strangest Matches

Tim Ward, Keith Wright and Clem Macintyre. I would also like to thank those who have chronicled the game's past. Finally, thanks to Anthea Matthison and Jeremy Robson at Robson Books.

Andrew Ward

THE ZULU WARRIORS

SHEFFIELD, NOVEMBER 1879

In January 1879 Cetewayo, the Zulu king, marshalled some 50,000 warriors to repel the British army's invasion of Zululand. The Zulu warriors fought with assegais, spears and ox-hide shields, and wore uniforms that were no more than a tuft of hair acting as a loin-cloth, but were well-organized and disciplined. The British completely underestimated them. After bloody battles at Isandhlwana and Rorke's Drift, it wasn't until August that the Zulu force was overcome. The British army lost over 1,300 men, about 1,000 natives and the French Prince Imperial, who was in their charge. Zulu loss of life was even greater. The Zulu War also heralded the breakdown of the Zulu kingdom. Cetewayo was captured, British Zululand was eventually handed over to the colony of Natal and it became part of the Republic of South Africa.

Just ten weeks after Wolseley's settlement had ended the Zulu War, a team of Zulu warriors arrived at Sheffield's Bramall Lane by hansom cab. They bore names like Cetewayo, the great king himself, Sirayo, a famous chieftain, and Dabulamanzi, Cetewayo's brother. They left their assegais and shields on the touchline, took on the best players in Sheffield, which was then the centre of world soccer, and beat them 5–4. Cetewayo, now in his 50s, did very well against Mosforth, the England international winger.

Perhaps I should point out that the Zulus were only Zulu in name. They were not black men but white soccer players,

1

faces and hands corked, bodies covered with black jerseys and stockings, feathers round their heads and white beads around their necks. The Sheffield players complained that some of the burnt cork rubbed off during the jostling in the match; they needed a better bath than normal.

The players were announced with Zulu names, but Dabula-manzi, for instance, was really Jack Hunter, one of the best Scottish players of the generation. The game was played to raise money for the widows and orphans of soldiers killed in the Zulu War, and a crowd of around 2,000 contributed to the cause. The Zulu warrior team, formed by Mr Brewer of Fargate, had already played one game, in Scarborough. Now, encouraged by the success in Sheffield, they began to tour the region, visiting places such as Barnsley and Chesterfield. It became an exhibition team, masquerading, experimenting more and more with warpaint, frolicking and clowning. They never lost a game.

After a few months the Sheffield FA began to disapprove. A storm broke when Jack Hunter was dropped from a North–South representative game because he had played in a Zulu game in Scotland. W. Pierce Dix of the Sheffield FA wrote to the local newspaper in January 1881 to explain the action: 'The Zulus were going about the country playing matches in a manner which in the opinion of the committee was calculated to degrade the game and bring discredit upon those connected with it; and further, that these players were receiving payment for playing.'

Zulu players were warned that they would be barred from representative games and FA Cup ties. The team disbanded. They hung up their assegais and shields for ever. The next year, Cetewayo visited London as part of his temporary exile. Dressed in European clothes, he was a popular figure with great authority, dignity and adaptability. In another life he might have made a football manager.

THE CROSSBAR PROTEST

LONDON, WINTER 1888

This was the year Crewe Alexandra reached an FA Cup semi-final. Along the way they played a strange match with the Swifts in Kensington.

Crewe reached the fourth round (the last 23) by beating Druids and Northwich Victoria. They had a bye in the third round, as would nine clubs in the fourth. After the game against the Swifts, which finished 2–2, Crewe claimed that one crossbar was two inches lower than the other and two inches below the height required by the rules. Swifts were disqualified from the competition and Crewe were through.

After this controversy, the Football Association passed a rule that protests about the ground, markings and goals must be made before the kick-off, not at the end of the game.

Crewe went on to beat Derby County in the fifth round and Middlesbrough in the sixth. Their semi-final opponents were Preston North End, then invincible. The game was played at Liverpool with a lake on the ground. It was really a game of water-polo. Crewe lost 4–0.

THE MYSTERY GAME

SHEFFIELD, AUGUST 1889

An FA Cup semi-final, played at Bramall Lane in 1889, sparked an idea. Several local soccer dignitaries decided to form a football section of the Sheffield United Cricket Club. Bramall Lane was big enough to take cricket and football.

At first it was a club without players. Advertisements in the local newspapers weren't especially successful – three players were acquired. Also, there were the first signs that the new club wouldn't be accepted easily. Sheffield Wednesday were already established. Other Sheffield clubs looked at Sheffield United suspiciously. The new club tactfully recruited outside Sheffield, relying particularly on Scotland. By the end of the summer Sheffield United had a team of assorted players, the best of whom turned out to be Howlett, a bespectacled goalkeeper from Gainsborough.

Sheffield United's first game was a mystery game. Whether this was because they were expecting trouble from rival clubs, or they were expecting the embarrassment of players not fitting in with one another immediately, is unclear. Nevertheless, the club gathered all the new players and sneaked away in a brake without telling anyone where they were going. They reckoned without the Sherlock Holmes qualities of one Sheffield reporter and Sheffield Wednesday captain Ted Brayshaw, both of whom succeeded in following the brake. They were able to reveal later that Sheffield United went to the Hallam Cricket Club where they lost 3–1 to Sheffield Football Club.

THE ONE-MAN TEAM

BURNLEY, DECEMBER 1891

Snow was falling heavily and it was one of the coldest weeks of the year. No one felt much like playing football. Certainly none of the Blackburn Rovers players did; but, being mainly professionals, they came out of the pavilion to take on Burnley.

Conceding three goals in the first 25 minutes did nothing to raise their spirits. Already it was a tetchy game. Two players squared up to each other in a bid to keep warm and settle a quarrel in the cold. When half-time arrived everybody was pleased.

The ten-minute interval passed. Burnley were on the field but there was no sign of Blackburn Rovers. The referee was the notorious J.C. Clegg from Sheffield, a high-ranking FA official and a man to stand no nonsense. Nor did he like waiting in the cold. He warned the teams that he would start in two minutes. In fact he waited four. Even then not all the Rovers players had returned to the pitch.

Soon tempers rose again. The two feuding players came to blows and were sent off. But what followed next was extraordinary. All the Blackburn players except goalkeeper Herby Arthur left the field. The referee, aware that he had done the correct thing by starting the game when there were more than six players, simply carried on. It was Burnley against the opposing goalkeeper.

Herby Arthur was nearing the end of his tremendous career with Blackburn Rovers. He had joined the club as a right-half in 1880, then volunteered to keep goal in the reserve team when a vacancy occurred with no obvious replacement. He played in Rovers' hat trick of FA Cup Final wins in the mid-1880s and became an established England international. Unlike most of the Rovers' players, he remained an amateur.

This was his biggest test. Burnley restarted the game and bore down on his goal.

'Offside,' yelled Herby Arthur.

It was given.

There followed an eternal period of time-wasting. Herby Arthur, with no one to pass the ball to, dallied as long as he could. Eventually the referee gave up and abandoned the game.

Blackburn Rovers later apologized, saying that their players were numb with cold and couldn't continue. Two days later Herby Arthur was given a benefit when Rovers played Sunderland.

THE TRUSTED GOALKEEPER

LONDON, MARCH 1892

When Aston Villa reached the 1892 FA Cup Final, one of the stars of the team was 27-year-old Jimmy Warner, a fine and trusted goalkeeper, one of the oldest players in the team. Five years earlier, Warner had kept goal so magnificently that many said he had won Villa the FA Cup. Now Villa were 7–4 favourites to win the FA Cup again . . . but the bookmakers reckoned without the strangest performance of Jimmy Warner's career.

Villa's short odds for the FA Cup Final were more than justified given their success in the League – they were pressing for the Championship. On the other hand, their Cup Final opponents, West Bromwich Albion, were languishing in the relegation zone.

A week before the Final, Villa flexed their muscles with a 12–2 win against Accrington. Then the team went to Holt Fleet for special training – running exercises, brine-baths at Droitwich and a spell of football practice every afternoon. On the Tuesday, when it snowed, the quick-thinking trainer moved the players into a 70-yard boat-shed and continued the preparations under cover.

Already, during this pre-Cup Final week, Jimmy Warner was being noticed. Not by players, or spectators, or the press, but by Villa committee members, who were monitoring their goalkeeper's activities. It was alleged that Warner would not go through the same training schedule as the other

7

players, and that instead of remaining with his team-mates he 'preferred the company of a certain person to whom the committee objected and who had actually been with him at Holt Fleet against the wish of the committee'.

On Cup Final day, there were about 30,000 people at Kennington Oval, some of them perched precariously on top of the mighty gas-holder. Most knew that on paper Aston Villa should win by a street.

In West Brom's first attack Jasper Geddes sent in a screw shot: 'Warner received it, but the ball seemed to spin out of his hands, and the first goal was scored for the Albion only three minutes from the start.'

It was later described in the press as a 'terrible blunder' but it looked likely to be academic when Villa swarmed to the West Brom end. Jimmy Cowan put a free-kick straight into the West Brom goal-net – nets were being used in a Cup Final for the first time – but as nobody touched the ball it didn't count as a goal, such were the rules of the day.

For 20 minutes Villa used the wind to stay on top, then Jimmy Warner had his second chance to shine: 'Warner partly muffed it, and Nicholls rushed up to send it through the posts.'

After half-time it was 2–0 to West Brom, against the wind, against the odds.

In the 55th minute West Brom's 'Baldy' Reynolds shot from 40 yards. Warner was hopelessly out of position. 3–0 to Albion.

Although Aston Villa dominated the rest of the game, they could not score. Reporters chose words like 'lamentable exhibition' to describe Jimmy Warner's afternoon's work, and Villa fans started their inquests. Attention switched to the Old College public house at Spring Hill, where Warner was the landlord. That evening supporters sought retribution by smashing all the windows in the pub.

A rumour spread. Warner had lost money on a big sporting bet, so the goalkeeper had thrown the FA Cup Final to recoup his money.

Warner vehemently denied this, saying he had bet £18 to £12 against West Brom winning, and an even £1 on them not scoring. Why would he want his business to suffer, his wife blackguarded and a mob threatening his pub? Show us your proof, declared Warner, who promised to give his accusers a good thrashing if necessary.

The next Wednesday, a few days before a vital League game with Sunderland, Warner failed to show for training. The next set of rumours claimed he had taken flight from his pub with a week's takings and a servant girl.

Fielding a deputy goalkeeper, Villa lost at Sunderland, finished fourth in the League and went down 2–0 to West Brom in the semi-final of the Birmingham Cup.

Jimmy Warner had played his last game for Aston Villa. The next season he showed up briefly with Newton Heath (later called Manchester United), no doubt thankful that not every newspaper had castigated him for his bizarre display in the Cup Final. 'Certainly he did fumble a lot with almost every shot he had to negotiate,' wrote one reporter, 'but I incline to the opinion that his backs were outclassed by the Albion forwards, and he, in consequence, was not so fully supported as he was wont to be.'

Perhaps.

THE GAME OF THREE HALVES

SUNDERLAND, SEPTEMBER 1894

On the first day of the 1894–5 soccer season Sunderland were at home to Derby County. The official referee, Mr Kirkham, was late. The game started with a deputy in charge, later named as John Conqueror of Southwick. The two teams played for 45 minutes and then Mr Kirkham arrived. What should he do?

Mr Kirkham made an incredible decision. He offered Derby County, who were losing 3–0, the option of starting again. Naturally they took it. Two more halves followed, and the game became known as 'the game of three halves'.

Derby were captained by England international John Goodall, who lost the toss twice. Derby were forced to kick against a strong gale for the first two halves. But the biggest panic was among the pressmen present at the game. They had already despatched messages all over the country to the effect that Sunderland were winning 3–0 at half-time. Fortunately, Derby obliged by conceding three more goals during the second first half.

Perversely, the decision to start the game *de novo* probably favoured Sunderland more than Derby. After kicking against the wind for 90 minutes the visiting players were, to say the least, weary. Sunderland scored five more in the third half. The result was recorded as an 8–0 win although Sunderland had scored 11 goals during the three halves. A pattern was set for the season. Sunderland sailed to their third Football

League Championship, while Derby were fortunate to hang on to their First Division status.

The 'game of three halves' assumed a legendary place among the folklore of Derby County players, none more than England-international goalkeeper Jack Robinson, who conceded 11 goals that afternoon. Robinson had previously boasted that he would never concede 10 goals in a game (adding as a joke that he would come out of goal when the opposition reached 9) and his team-mates debated whether the Sunderland game counted as 8 or 11. Robinson explained the debacle by his failure to eat rice pudding before the match at Sunderland – the only time he missed with his superstition. 'No pudding, no points,' Robinson would tell his team-mates, who would go to great lengths to indulge their temperamental goalkeeper. One day at Burnley, when a hotel waitress announced the rice pudding was 'off', John Goodall went searching for an hour before he came up with a plate of something which would pass for the same dish. Derby County won at Burnley that day, and they played just two halves.

THE FOUR-MINUTE GAME

STOKE, DECEMBER 1894

Referees have discretionary powers to suspend or terminate a game whenever they deem it necessary. In Britain, the reason is usually the weather, although referees are advised to give the matter very careful consideration before yielding to the elements. Otherwise there would be very little soccer played. I know of one Football League game – Grimsby Town against Oldham Athletic in 1909 – where weather conditions *twice* caused an abandonment. Over a period of seven weeks these two teams met three times and played almost 220 minutes of soccer. Grimsby won 2–0 after trailing by a goal in the second game.

Among the candidates for the shortest-ever game must be the occasion Stoke City entertained Wolverhampton Wanderers in a blinding snowstorm. The weather was so bad that only about 300 or 400 people turned up to watch. Play immediately proved farcical. The referee, Mr Helme, decided to abandon the game after four minutes (some sources say three). The storm soon cleared but the wind persisted, and the conditions were unbearable for spectators and players. For the record, Stoke won the toss.

STRIKE TACTICS IN THE DRESSING-ROOM

WALSALL, DECEMBER 1894

It was a precarious season for Walsall Town Swifts. Crowds were small, income minimal, and the players were fed up with not being paid. They sat in the dressing-room and discussed financial matters with the club's committee: no wages, no game.

Outside the crowd gathered, if you could call it a crowd. Supporters had been patient all season – Walsall were third from bottom of Division Two – and now they needed even more patience. Kick-off time came and went. Walsall's opponents, Newcastle United, stayed in the dressing-room and waited, listening to the hail and sleet beating down on the roof.

The matter was resolved to some degree, and the game started 20 minutes late. Walsall kicked uphill towards most of the mud. They soon had Newcastle down to ten men but didn't make much impact on the score. Newcastle rattled in three goals and led 3–0 at half-time.

In the second half Walsall Town Swifts scored twice and had a chance of saving the game. The main stumbling block was that there was so much weather about – sleet and hail, rain and gale. The referee abandoned the game after 78 minutes with Newcastle still 3–2 ahead. The Football League later ruled that the result should stand, even though Walsall were pressing for an equalizer when the referee made his decision not to proceed.

The next Monday Walsall sacked five of their first-team players. The others were asked to play for expenses plus a pittance until the club hit better times. Somehow the club tottered on till the end of the season, when they lost their Football League status to Loughborough Town.

NOT ONE SHOT AT GOAL

STOKE, APRIL 1898

Modern-day soccer may have its highly developed defensive strategies and across-the-field build-up, but the strangest shot-shy game of all took place more than 90 years go, when Stoke City and Burnley engineered a goalless draw to save their places in the First Division.

Stoke and Burnley were engaged with two other teams (Newcastle and Blackburn) in a series of test matches to decide promotion and relegation between the two divisions. On the morning of the final round of matches, Stoke and Burnley were joint top of the mini-league. A draw would suit them both, but it didn't suit the 4,000 people who braved torrential rain and strong wind to attend the game at Stoke's Victoria Ground.

It was a fiasco. The goalkeepers hardly touched the ball, passes went to opponents when either team looked well-placed to attack, and, if a forward did by chance find himself in a shooting position he would aim at the corner-flag. Players' kit remained surprisingly clean in the atrocious conditions, and the best chance of a goal was a tame back-pass.

The crowd quickly realized what was happening. They booed and jeered, or, for variation, cheered sarcastically. They shouted kind words of advice.

'Come off the field, we're doing more than you!'

'Play the game!'

'Them goal-nets were invented for a reason.'

As the second half progressed, still no goals, still no shots at goal, the crowd on the Boothen Road side of the ground began to make their own entertainment. When the ball was kicked into their small wooden stand, they hung on to it. To their utter disgust another ball appeared. Undaunted, however, they tried again, and again, and again. This small section of the crowd spent most of the second half trying to stop the game by keeping all the footballs. They put one on top of the grandstand and another in the River Trent. Five balls were used altogether, but the game continued to its bitter goalless end.

The crowd's game within a game did lead to the day's best action. A linesman sprinted along the touchline in a bid to catch a ball before it went into the crowd. A perambulating policeman had his eye on the same ball. The linesman collided with the policeman and they lay spreadeagled across the track. The crowd roared, but only with laughter.

The result was never in doubt. Stoke City retained their First Division status and Burnley were promoted from Division Two. Poor Newcastle United, whose players were showing much more effort in defeating Blackburn, finished third in the mini-league, a point behind Stoke and Burnley.

Perhaps one interesting question is how the goalless draw was arranged such that the players trusted one another. Among the participants were experienced Jimmy Ross, who played in five successive test-match series (for Preston, Liverpool and Burnley), and most interestingly, Jack 'Happy Jack' Hillman, the burly and brilliant Burnley goalkeeper, whose career was always within a whisker of controversy and comedy.

Hillman, a Devonian by birth, played for Burnley and Everton before a two-season spell with Dundee. During his second season with the Scottish club Hillman was suspended for not trying, which was why he came to Burnley for £130 in time to help them into the First Division. Hillman was then in his late-20s, but much was still to happen to him. He played a game for England, and was twice suspended by the FA – for a season (1900–01) after allegedly bribing Nottingham Forest players to lose to Burnley, and for eight months (1906–07) for receiving illegal payments as a Manchester City player.

Jack Hillman had once won a bet that he could keep goal in a charity match with one hand tied behind his back and not concede a goal. At Stoke, on that farcical goalless afternoon, he had no need to handle the ball at all. Indeed, he had already bet someone that he would not concede four goals in Burnley's four test matches. He had let in three before the Stoke stroll and there was no chance of a fourth going past him that afternoon.

The Stoke-Burnley game goes down in history on two counts. The authority's disgust at the players' actions led to the curtailing of test matches in favour of automatic promotion and relegation, and, secondly, as far as I am aware, it is the only game without a shot at goal played at the highest levels. There have been games where teams have settled for a result by mutual consent, notably West Germany's 1–0 win over Austria, which enabled both countries to progress to the next group of the 1982 World Cup Finals, and the relegation-escaping 2–2 draw between Coventry and Bristol City in 1977; and there have always been goalless games which tested spectators' patience. When Chelsea met Portsmouth in an end-of-season goalless bore in 1932, the highlight of the game was when the ball burst. 'The ball's packed up,' shouted one spectator. 'Why don't you do the same?'

Any survivors from the Stoke-Burnley pantomime would have sympathized.

COMPLETED – FIFTEEN WEEKS LATER

SHEFFIELD, NOVEMBER 1898, MARCH 1899

At half-time on a drab November Saturday, Argus-Jud, a Birmingham press-man, bet a Sheffield reporter a cigar and a cognac that the game wouldn't be completed. He won his bet – the game was abandoned ten minutes from time – but the Sheffield man might have felt he had cause for a refund when he heard the Football League's decision. In the 1890s each abandoned game was treated on its merits rather than automatically replayed. For some, the score was allowed to stand. For others, as in the case of this Sheffield Wednesday– Aston Villa game, the game had to be completed at a later date.

The problems started when the match referee, Aaron Scragg, a Crewe fuel agent and FA Councillor, missed his Manchester train connection by ten seconds. He telegraphed to the Sheffield Wednesday offices, but these were some distance from Wednesday's ground. By kick-off time (2.30 pm) no one knew where the referee was.

The game started seven minutes late. A local Football League referee, Fred Bye, took charge until Aaron Scragg arrived at half-time. About 17,000 were present, a good-sized crowd considering Wednesday were on the slide and the weather was dire. It had rained all morning and a keen, piercing wind blew towards the Heeley end. The ground was heavy and the ball fell dead at times. It was also very, very gloomy.

18

Wednesday took the lead after 20 minutes, Crawshaw's shot hitting the legs of three or four defenders and zigzagging into the net. Aston Villa equalized a minute later. Frank Bedingfield, a late replacement at centre-forward, hooked Smith's centre into the net. It was the only Football League goal Bedingfield would ever score. Three years later he collapsed after playing an FA Cup-tie for Portsmouth and he died of consumption in South Africa not long afterwards.

A goal by Dryburgh gave Wednesday a 2–1 half-time lead. The next goal – Hemmingfield's header giving Wednesday a 3–1 lead – was awarded by match-referee Aaron Scragg, who had finally found his way to the ground. But Scragg's difficulties continued. The pitch was in semi-darkness. Players tried to spot the white shorts or striped shirts that weren't too muddy. Spectators listened for the sounds of players shouting. Some could see the ball only when it was punted above the level of the stands.

There were just over ten minutes left to play when protests by Devey of Aston Villa led to Aaron Scragg consulting a linesman. The game was abandoned and the debate began. Wednesday claimed that their 3–1 lead was the springboard for almost certain victory and they should be awarded the game. Reporters agreed that, from what they could see, Villa looked very unlikely to recover. On the other hand, Villa claimed Wednesday were to blame for arranging such a late kick-off; they should have known November days were gloomy, and therefore the whole match should be replayed.

The Football League, in their wisdom, compromised. They decided the extra ten-and-a-bit minutes should be played on a convenient date. So the game continued . . . 15 weeks later.

One conundrum was how to start the game. Would Aaron Scragg remember where the ball was when he abandoned the game, so that he could drop it from the right place?

A second conundrum was the eligibility of players. Would the same 22 men be forced to resume their places?

A third problem was the likely low attendance. Who would turn out to watch the last ten minutes of a game when the result was cut-and-dried?

19

The Football League ruled that play would start in the usual manner – tossing a coin for choice of ends and then a place-kick – and that any registered player could take part. In the event, Villa used 13 players and Wednesday 16. No doubt the club secretary needed an abacus to decide how the win bonus would be divided.

Someone had a bright idea to entice the crowd. After the ten-minute farce, the two teams would play a 90-minute friendly (provided the light held good). The proceeds of the friendly would go to Wednesday's Harry Davis, whose benefit match a few weeks before was very badly attended. (On this occasion 3,000 people turned up and Wednesday beat Villa 2–0.)

For 15 weeks Wednesday had desperately needed the two points held in abeyance. Relegation was probable, whereas Villa were favourites for the League Championship. During the infamous 630 seconds of the replay, Wednesday added a further goal to make it a 4–1 victory, but it didn't keep them in the First Division. Villa won the Championship.

This was not the only Football League game to be completed at a later date – Stoke were once ordered to Wolverhampton to play five minutes, and Walsall and Newton Heath completed on a second day – but it proved to be the last. Such was the adverse publicity that the Football League changed its rules over abandoned matches.

THE PENALTY-KICKING ELEPHANT

LEICESTER, LATE 1890s

Sanger's Circus was in town. They had an elephant who was unbeaten in penalty-kick competitions. When the circus proprietor issued a challenge to Leicester Fosse professional footballers – no one can beat our elephant – it was a challenge too good to miss. Four Leicester Fosse players accepted and took on the elephant.

For each competition the player and the elephant would take four penalties each. The ball, it must be said, favoured the elephant. It was about six times the size of a normal football.

Three of the four Fosse players lost to the elephant. The last hope was William Keech, who used a crafty penalty-taking technique. Keech feinted to play the ball one side of the elephant, then, as the elephant raised its foot in anticipation, Keech slotted the ball into the other corner. The elephant had met a worthy opponent, but hung on to draw 2–2. A replay was ordered. This time Keech's deceptions were too much for the elephant, who went under 3–2.

So, if you ever get around to picking a team from the animal kingdom to play one of those world teams selected in the back of a football autobiography, please don't forget about the elephant. He may not have much mobility but, with a spot of training, could warrant a place on the substitutes' bench, just in case the game should go to a penalty shoot-out.

A TEMPESTUOUS SEMI-FINAL

NOTTINGHAM, BOLTON, MANCHESTER AND DERBY, MARCH 1899

Willie Foulke, goalkeeper for England and Sheffield United (and later Chelsea), was probably the largest footballer ever. He started his career at 15 stone and ended it at 22 stone. Well over six feet tall, he dwarfed players and became a legend with his variable moods.

Talk about strength. Foulke could easily carry a man under each arm. He could punch a football to the halfway-line. And talk about girth. The ground rumbled and the stadium darkened when he came out to narrow the angle, an exceedingly difficult man to put the ball past. He was big enough to save penalties without doing too much, as, in his day, goalkeepers were allowed to advance when penalty-kicks were being taken.

Willie Foulke was also legendary at giving away penalties. On one occasion he picked up a forward around the waist and threw him into the net to concede a penalty. Another time, during a League game in the 1898–9 season, he picked up Liverpool centre-forward George Allan, turned him upside-down and stood him on his head in the mud. The resultant penalty turned the game Liverpool's way.

Imagine, then, the effect of the semi-final draw later that same season: Liverpool against Sheffield United. George Allan against Willie Foulke.

Foulke was in great form that year. On one occasion he

kept Sheffield United in the FA Cup competition with a brilliant save but tore a thigh muscle in the process. The stretchers weren't big enough to carry him off. It needed six men instead.

He was fit enough for the semi-final. The first attempt was at Nottingham. Hedley gave Sheffield United the lead. The equalizer, from Foulke's old adversary Allan, was inevitably greeted with a surly glare. Morgan gave Liverpool a half-time lead. Sheffield United rescued a 2–2 draw with a goal from Walter 'Cocky' Bennett.

The next attempt to settle the tie, at Bolton, had twice as many goals. Twice Liverpool were two goals ahead (2–0 and 4–2) but two goals in the last eight minutes by Priest saved Sheffield United. Allan again scored one of the Liverpool goals.

The third game was at Fallowfield. The crowd invaded the pitch and played their own game. During the 90-minute first half – half the time spent clearing the pitch – Allan gave Liverpool the lead and there was the much-anticipated clash between Foulke and the goalscorer. The Liverpool centre-forward, a hotheaded Scottish international, was nothing but a nuisance to the Sheffield United goalkeeper.

Foulke had the last laugh of that semi-final. The Fallowfield game was abandoned at half-time, and Sheffield United won the fourth attempt, 1–0 at Derby. The Cup Final, by comparison to the semi-final, was an afternoon out. Sheffield United won the trophy by beating Derby County 4–1.

Altogether Willie Foulke played in three FA Cup Finals for Sheffield United, winning two and losing one. After the game at Crystal Palace in 1902, Foulke was incensed at the decision to allow Southampton's goal, scored late in the game by Harry Wood. Lying in the bath, contemplating the replay, his temper snapped with typical idiosyncracy. He stormed out of the dressing-area and stalked the Crystal Palace corridors in search of the referee and linesmen, twenty stones of steaming nudity. It must have been one of the strangest sights of the century.

SOCCER SICKNESS

LIVERPOOL, JANUARY 1902

The Stoke City management made a serious tactical error before the game at Liverpool – they allowed all the players to eat plaice for lunch. After the half-time interval in the game, only seven Stoke players were fit to resume. The Stoke secretary, Mr Austerberry, was very sympathetic. He was as sick as any of them.

Stoke goalkeeper Dick Roose was in distress before the game started. Roose, a Welsh international, was known as an adventurous goakeeper whose tactics of wandering all over the field were not curbed until the 1912 change of law. On this day Roose could think only of wandering *off* the field . . . as quickly as possible. He lasted just ten minutes, by when Stoke were a goal behind.

'Who wants to go in goal, lads? Come on, someone will have to go in.'

Meredith was the unlucky Stoke player appointed as deputy goalkeeper. For the rest of the first half, during which time he conceded three goals, Meredith made frantic gestures to indicate he would be happier out of goal. His captain, Johnstone, merely flashed back encouraging smiles.

At half-time the busiest man in the dressing-room was Dr Moody, a Stoke director, who examined most of the players and detected signs of lead poisoning. Moody had made his own way to the ground and had therefore escaped the midday meal.

Roose and Ashworth were the most afflicted of the Stoke players, and it was apparent that they would take no further part in the match. Dr Moody also recommended that Watkins and Whitehouse remain in the dressing-room. The only two people in the Stoke party seemingly unaffected were the two trainers, who had passed over the fish at lunch-time.

Dr Moody was left in no doubt about the seriousness of the illnesses. He said later: 'In fact the dressing-room resembled the cabin of a cross-Channel steamer in bad weather, and smelt like it . . . only more so.'

Stoke started the second half with seven players. They played with a goalkeeper – still Meredith – one back, two halves and three forwards. And did quite well too. There was a short spell when Liverpool failed to score.

While people were beginning to debate at what point the game might be abandoned, the two missing forwards, Watkins and Whitehouse, gallantly reappeared against doctor's orders. Goalkeeper Roose, meanwhile, who had a pulse-rate of 148 per minute when he left the field, would need a few hours rest to recover.

In his absence Liverpool scored some soft goals. Not until the sixth went in did Meredith have his wish granted; Clarke took over in goal.

The final total was seven. Not Stoke's favourite number. They had seven fit men, conceded seven goals . . . and lost the next seven games.

FISHERMEN VERSUS FIREMEN

SCARBOROUGH, DECEMBER 1905

The game between the fishermen and engineer deck-hands of Scarborough and district steam trawlers was an annual fixture in the 1900s. It took place on Boxing Day, providing a festive focus for Scarborough people, many of whom gave generously to charity.

The venue was Scarborough's South Sands. Goalposts were sunk in barrels, top hats were worn, and a procession of decorated tramcars paraded through the main streets on the morning of the match. The Rifle Volunteer Band played selections of music as the firemen and fishermen played selections of football. In 1905, the fishermen won 5–3, but the firemen made amends by winning the tug-of-war competition held afterwards.

The 1905 game was particularly important because the remarkably fine weather helped produce record receipts. The proceeds of the game were handed over to two widows. The deceased men were John Lancaster, a well-known Scarborough cobleman, and Robert Thompson, who had been prominent in local footballing circles.

This unusually large gathering of trawlermen also provided the opportunity for other business. Burton Truefitt, a fisherman on a Hartlepool trawler, was presented with a gold watch to commemorate an occasion when he attempted to rescue a colleague at sea, diving into the seas in his oil-skins, returning to the boat to remove clothing and diving again.

The gold watch contained the following inscription: 'Presented to Burton Truefitt for his heroic attempt to save the life of the late George Whittleton who was drowned at sea, September 23rd 1905, from the steam trawler St Mary.'

UNDER THE SCORCHING SUN

MANCHESTER, SEPTEMBER 1906

At half-time Manchester City players could talk only of the sun, those who could still talk. Outside it was more than 90 degrees fahrenheit in the shade – too hot for sunbathing. There had been no forewarning of the unbearable heat for the newcomers to the City team, especially the Scottish imports, and it was virtually a new-look team because 17 City players and ex-players had recently been suspended by the FA. On the first day of the season, City were sunshocked and shellshocked.

Harry Newbould was the new secretary-manager of Manchester City – several officials had also been suspended after the FA inquiry into financial affairs – and he must have been desolate when he saw the dressing-room scene at half-time. City were 2–0 down to Woolwich Arsenal, three players looked incapable of continuing and it was 60 years before the use of substitutes. Thornley and Grieve were flat on their backs, too ill with sunstroke to do any more work that day. Little Jimmy Conlin, who had sensibly taken the field with a handkerchief tied over his head, had been forced to take refuge in the dressing-room a few minutes before half-time. City were down to eight men.

In Harry Newbould's day, managers were not the strategic conjurors and media magic-men that they are today. Their role was mainly to sign players, pin up team-sheets and ensure the players were all in the right railway carriage.

Newbould was one of the more enterprising of his ilk, and at half-time he might have had some say about tactics on that scorching day. Translated into more modern managerial hype, the message conveyed to the City players would have been something like this: 'Right, lads, I know it was a bad toss to lose, and it's not the best of conditions, but we'll have the sun on our backs this second half and it'll be the same for them. It's only eleven of them against eight of us. No, Bill, it won't be like this every week in Manchester. Okay, lads, we're two down, and we've only got eight men, but we can go out and take the game to them. I want us to· play a 1–3–3 formation this half. That's one full-back, three half-backs and three forwards. And we'll try to catch them offside. Yes, I know you don't know each other very well and only a couple of you have played for City before, but look at it this way, it'll be easier to get to know seven others than ten others. This is a great chance for a good start to the season. And, remember, if you hear the crowd cheering, they're cheering for you, not because they've seen the sun in Manchester.'

Whatever Newbould or anybody else actually said at half-time, it certainly did the trick. Even though City had lost three forwards with sunstroke, they pushed a defender into the forward-line and played a 1–3–3 formation. In the 50th minute Jimmy Conlin returned to the field and the crowd cheered as if they'd seen the sun for the first time.

Taking his position in what was now a 1–3–4 formation, Conlin made a goal for Dorsett, and City, only 2–1 down, were back in the game. But that was as far as it went. Dorsett collapsed soon afterwards, the heat struck down Kelso and Buchan, and City were down to five fit men plus the plucky Conlin.

The referee spoke to his linesmen, but they agreed that there was no just cause for abandoning the game. The Woolwich Arsenal players, meanwhile, were far less affected. They scored two more goals, taking the score to 4–1, but sportingly didn't cash in too much when they faced five fit men in the closing stages of the game.

It took City some time to recover from this setback – two days later they lost 9–1 at Everton – but the new-look team pulled together sufficiently to keep the club in the First Division.

NOT ACCORDING TO THE RULES

BUDAPEST, MAY 1908

Manchester United's positive approach to the European Cup in the mid-1950s has set the club apart as a European pioneer in Britain. There are fewer references to United's European pacesetting in the 1900s. Their month-long tour of Europe in May 1908 took the team to Switzerland, France, Germany, Austria, Belgium and Hungary. On the whole everyone enjoyed the tour and voted it a success, but there was some slight bother in Hungary towards the end. United's management, on returning to England, said it would never take the club to Budapest again. (Things had obviously changed by 1965, when Manchester United drew Ferencvaros in an Inter-Cities Fairs' Cup semi-final.)

On 24 May 1908, two days after they had beaten a team drawn from the best of three Hungarian clubs 6–2, United played Ferencvaro si Tornaklub and won by seven clear goals. There are different accounts of what caused the riot.

Apparently the referee wished to send off three Manchester United players for infringing Hungarian rules. The United players tried to explain British rules to the referee, who spoke no English. In doing so, one or two players put hands on the referee's shoulders. A section of the 11,000 crowd interpreted this as an attack. Stones flew through the air. Police intervened. United were grateful that only one player was hit by a stone; he ended the game with a bruise on his head.

31

Some reports suggested that the teams dined together after the game, but this was later denied. The United team were clear that they considered their lives too precious to risk a visit to Budapest again, and their management supported them. They blamed both the Hungarian players – 'they go for the man and not the ball,' said secretary-manager Mangnall – and the referee, who didn't understand English rules and couldn't speak English. Such comments probably did little to help English teams overcome their xenophobia.

It took Hungary nearly 50 years to gain respect in Britain for their soccer, and then it happened in the most emphatic manner possible. In 1953, Hungary, 6–3 winners at Wembley, became the first country to beat England on their home soil. A Dutch referee ensured that both teams were playing to the same rules.

THE SURPRISE LOCAL DERBY

NEWCASTLE, DECEMBER 1908

The first outstanding team of the 20th century was Newcastle United. In a eight-year period centring on the late 1900s, Newcastle won the League Championship three times and reached five FA Cup Finals, winning the trophy once. The Newcastle team of all talents contained England internationals like the versatile Colin Veitch and winger Jackie Rutherford, star Scottish internationals such as wing-half Peter McWilliam, goalkeeper Jimmy Lawrence and winger George Wilson, and Irish-international full-back wizard Bill McCracken. No team relished going to St James Park to play against the unruffled, unrivalled Newcastle United, a team with the prestige of a modern-day Liverpool, which makes the events of 5 December 1908 so astounding.

It was a local derby game. Newcastle (second in Division One) were at home to Sunderland (sixth). At half-time the score was 1–1. Newcastle, having just equalized with a penalty, were expected to take control after the break. Instead something incredible happened. In the space of 28 second-half minutes Sunderland scored EIGHT, repeat EIGHT times. The final result was 9–1.

The pitch was heavy, and Newcastle, experimenting with their team, included three players who played very little in the first team that season. There was no McCracken in the team, no McWilliam and no Rutherford, Even so, Sunderland's performance was remarkable by any standards. Billy

33

Hogg scored four, George Holley three and Arthur Bridgett two. Every shot was a winner during the second-half storm.

That season Newcastle United won the League Championship by seven points, and Sunderland finished third.

THE CIRCUS GAME

BIRKENHEAD, AUTUMN 1910

There is a particular breed of professional footballer who frowns on people tinkering with the rules of the game. Circus acts belong in the circus, he may say when he discovers a lighthearted experiment at a village fête or local sports. A team once entered a five-a-side competition wearing gorilla suits. Unfortunately one player collapsed with breathing difficulties.

One excellent example of the 'circus game' was that at a village sports near Birkenhead in 1910. A match was arranged between two teams with different handicaps. One team had their arms tied to their sides and their boots and stockings removed. The players of the other team were mounted on stilts, six feet high.

A report in *Thomson's Weekly News* summarized the play: 'The contest was not so unequal as might have been expected for, though those on stilts found it difficult to touch the ball, their antagonists discovered how important a part the arms play in maintaining balance, and when they attempted to run they fell in all directions. In the end the tied arm team won.'

Personally I am not convinced. I am sure I would rather play in a tied arm team than on six-foot stilts, and I wouldn't want to be responsible for anybody who tried to prove me wrong.

THE 'TONYPANDEMONIUM' GAME

TONYPANDY, NOVEMBER 1910

They called it 'Tonypandemonium' when striking South Wales coal-miners rioted and Home Secretary Winston Churchill sent in troops, but the civil unrest had barely died down when the soldiers played the strikers at football.

On Monday 31 October about 12,000 Tonypandy coal-miners downed tools. The four pits involved were members of the Cambrian combine. A week later pickets answered a bugle call at 4 am and took to the streets in force. They posted themselves at every street corner and at the entrances to each of the four Cambrian collieries.

The pickets' violence against the collieries included raking the fires from the boilers and stoning the buildings, but that was small-scale compared with the events of Tuesday evening. Shop windows were smashed and the contents were looted.

Troops were called in. A detachment of the North Lancashire Regiment arrived on the Wednesday evening. Less than a week later Major-General Macready reported that order was restored. His report contained a small reference to the evidence of normality: 'A football match between the strikers and the soldiers was played at Tonypandy in which the soldiers were victorious.'

'Pray consult me on any points which cause you embarrassment,' replied Winston Churchill.

The match in question took place on 15 November at the mid-Rhondda ground. The Lancashire Fusiliers, by far the better team, beat mid-Rhondda Athletic 4–1. Each goal was cheered heartily.

THE ELECTION CAMPAIGN GAME

MIDDLESBROUGH, DECEMBER 1910

Middlesbrough's home match with top-of-the-table Sunderland was scheduled for two days before the 1910 General Election. Middlesbrough chairman Colonel F. Gibson Poole, twice mayor of Middlesbrough, was standing as Unionist candidate for the local constituency. The incumbent Member of Parliament, Penry Williams, a Liberal, was favourite to be returned. Colonel Gibson Poole needed all the extra support he could muster. A good win against neighbours Sunderland might swing a few votes.

The key incident, as revealed to an FA Commission later, took place before the match. It was alleged that Middlesbrough's secretary-manager, Andy Walker, approached Charlie Thomson, Sunderland's Scottish international captain, offering £30 – £10 for Thomson, £2 for each of his team-mates – and saying it was for the colonel's sake, as it would make a big difference to Monday's election. The news of this approach soon spread through Sunderland's ranks – from captain to trainer to a director to the chairman, who reported it to the Football Association. An FA Commission later agreed that an illegal approach had been made. Colonel Gibson Poole and Andy Walker were suspended permanently. A separate FA Commission investigated the Middlesbrough club in more detail and found 'distinct and flagrant tampering with the books' that same season.

There are two results to announce. On the Saturday, Middlesbrough won by a single goal, scored in the first half when they had the wind behind them. In the second half, they hung on and defended desperately.

On the Monday, Colonel Gibson Poole went down by 3,745 votes, a slightly increased majority for Penry Williams, mainly because there was no Labour candidate at this election. Or perhaps the 1–0 victory just wasn't enough.

I have no details on the voting, but Nicholl scored the goal.

DEATH OF A REFEREE

WATTSTOWN, MARCH 1912

The valleys of South Wales have never been an easy territory for soccer referees – heavy, muddy grounds, intense rivalry, fervent supporters and players who usually had their origins in a rugged coal-mining environment. The old chestnut about what's in the game for referees – a small match fee, expenses and a decent funeral – turns sour when we consider the case of William Ernest Williams of Porth, near Pontypridd.

On 15 March 1912 Williams refereed a game at Wattstown, where Aberaman Athletic were the visitors. After the game Williams was brutally attacked while washing himself in the dressing-room. He died as a result of his injuries.

The player responsible, Hansford of Wattstown, was arrested and remanded for trial. He was sentenced to a month's imprisonment for manslaughter.

Several months later, Williams's mother attempted to recover £200 from the South Wales and Monmouthshire FA in an action under the Workmen's Compensation Act. The case, heard at Pontypridd County Court (January 1913), ruled that the referee's contract with the Association was not a contract of service and, anyway, he was paid by the clubs, not the Association. Had the referee been killed *during* the game, however, it might have been a different story.

BATTLE AT HALF-TIME

BELFAST, SEPTEMBER 1912

Revolvers and knives, sticks and stones, fists and feet. All were used in the battle at Celtic Park. At half-time the Belfast Celtic pitch was a seething mass of struggling men, the police unable to cope.

The riot started suddenly, but many people suspected that it was premeditated. Celtic Park was a Roman Catholic preserve. Linfield, Belfast Celtic's opponents that day, was another Belfast club but with a Protestant following.

Once on the pitch, the crowd split into two factions, one carrying a Union Jack, the other displaying the Belfast Celtic colours of green and white. Thousands were involved in the riot, and the police were swept away in the battle. The din was deafening.

For a time it appeared that people would be killed, but everyone survived the day. The nearby hospital worked overtime to deal with the 100 people who were injured, treating gunshot wounds, fractured skulls and facial injuries.

Hardly anyone was neutral, but if we had to trust a judgement we might rely on the match referee more than others. Mr J.H. Holmes told his story to the newspaper: 'Everything went right to the interval, when, before we could realize it, the pandemonium broke out. We were in the dressing-room at the time, and the officials and players were virtually prisoners. Even when the police reinforcements arrived we were unable to leave, although no attempt was made to molest the club officials or myself. We had a rough time, however, as the departing rioters made a fierce attack on the dressing-room, absolutely wrecking it. The gate money was in an inner room, and even this for a time was in jeopardy, the officials pushing a drawer which contained it against the door as a barricade, which fortunately held good until the rioters passed. During the hottest part of the siege the officials crouched behind, expecting every moment to be struck by stones or overwhelmed by the crowd. We had four policemen laid out in a room at once.'

The riot raged for more than half an hour. There was no hope of restarting the game, which was abandoned at half-time with Linfield leading by a single goal, scored neatly by Smith from McEwen's centre after half an hour's play. It was the only neat thing that happened at Belfast's Celtic Park that afternoon.

THE TEAM AWARDED FOUR PENALTIES

BURNLEY, FEBRUARY 1913

It is hard to imagine that the FA Cup competition passed through the first 20 years of its existence without the concept of the penalty-kick. Then, in a quarter-final game at Trent Bridge in 1891, Notts County's Hendry fisted out a shot that was obviously going through the goal. Opponents Stoke lost 1–0 because the laws had no just punishment for such an offence. Penalty-kicks, along the lines of those recently introduced in Ireland, were suggested.

Amateurs objected, arguing that the presence of a penalty-kick law implied a slur upon their moral behaviour on the field and might even encourage unsportsmanlike behaviour. For many years amateur players refused to recognize the penalty-kick law. If the Corinthians conceded a penalty their goalkeeper would stand by a goalpost until it had been taken.

When the penalty-kick was first introduced, goalkeepers were permitted to advance six yards from their goal-line. Some were especially quick off the mark and looked likely to reach the ball before the penalty-taker. In the early 1900s players began to counter by lifting the ball over the head of the advancing goalkeeper. Since 1905 a new law has restricted goalkeepers from moving from the goal-line. (Two more amendments were brought in in the 1920s – one to stop goalkeepers moving their feet, after a trend of off-putting

43

ape-like gestures from 'keepers, and one to introduce the ten-yard arc to stop teams lining a ten-man phalanx along the edge of the penalty area and thus restricting the taker's run-up to six yards.)

These were the circumstances, therefore, when Scott of Grimsby Town faced up to four Burnley penalty-kicks on 13 February 1909. The game was played on a very heavy ground and Grimsby suffered two early setbacks. First, Abbott put Burnley ahead. Next, Grimsby lost the injured Lee and had to play the last 70 minutes with ten men.

At first Grimsby played the one-back formation, the old-time equivalent of a sweeper. This was tantamount to setting an offside trap – in those days three defenders rather than two had to be behind the attacker – and made things difficult for Burnley. Even so, Scott broke free and was tripped by Henderson – the first penalty. Scott made a fine save.

Next Wheelhouse handled – the second penalty. Smith took the kick and again Scott moved quickly to make a good save. The Grimsby goalkeeper also saved the follow-up shot but in the resultant scramble somebody handled – the third penalty. Up stepped Abbott, who relieved Burnley supporters by giving his team a 2–0 half-time lead. Two out of three penalties saved, one scored.

After half-time Grimsby abandoned their one-back game in favour of a more orthodox defence and four forwards. They were reduced to nine players when Whitehouse left the field for 'repairs to his knickers' and while he was absent Davidson fouled Abbott – the fourth penalty.

Goalkeeper Scott was still on a hat-trick of penalty saves. Abbott made it easy for him. He shot straight at the goalkeeper. Scott's three penalty saves was a remarkable performance. In the last two months the goalkeeper had saved seven of eight penalties he had faced. Grimsby supporters feared that the defence might recklessly concede penalties, secure in the knowledge that Scott would save them – a mistaken belief, as it proved.

THE WAR GAME

NO MAN'S LAND, DECEMBER 1914

The trench warfare of World War One was bloody and slaughterous. British and German soldiers climbed from their respective trenches and charged at each other with murderous abandon. British troops would go over the top with a battle-cry, singing, or, in the case of the East Surrey Regiment on at least one occasion, kicking a football.

Deep down, however, many soldiers knew they were fighting a politicians' war. At times the soldiers at the front had sympathy for each other. From the safety of their trenches they might hold shouted conversations, words travelling across No Man's Land, some of the Germans understanding and speaking English. The conversation could easily turn to football – some Germans had been in England before the war – and the most natural thing for men to do was to challenge each other to a game.

There might have been more contests had footballs always been available. The game most frequently mentioned was that on Christmas Day 1914, when British and German soldiers met in No Man's Land to play their international match. The next day they were fighting again.

ONE-ARMED MEN VERSUS WOMEN

READING, SEPTEMBER 1917

Here was a game strange on four counts. Women played against men; the opposing teams were English and Canadian; the men played with hands behind their backs; and the final score was 8–5.

Perhaps the oddest thing was that men were allowed to play against the women on a Southern League ground. After an early wave of women's soccer in the late 1890s, inspired by the Rational Dress movement and generally believed to be organized by Nettie Honeyball in England and Lady Florence Dixie in Scotland, the FA Council (on 25 August 1902) issued instructions not to permit matches against 'lady teams'. This policy of separation – men against men, women against women – has continued ever since.

That didn't stop women copying men. In the mid-1900s, six-a-side soccer on roller-skates was introduced for men at Brighton skating-rink, and women soon took up the sport. The goals – 6 ft high and 7 ft wide – were larger than ice-hockey goals, and a regulation-size football containing a pint of water (to keep it from rising) was used. Players were allowed two minutes for skate-repair.

In World War One, with men away in the forces and women in Britain adopting male roles, there was a boom in women's soccer. Although the most lasting development of this period was the Dick-Kerr's factory team in Preston, there were spontaneous outbreaks all over the country, usually based around factories.

The standard picked up enormously. Back in 1895, 'Lady Correspondent' of the *Manchester Guardian* had been gently scathing about how well the North and South players knocked the ball about: 'They danced around the ball when they reached it as if uncertain what to do with it, much after the manner of a lapdog which has accidentally laid hold of the cat which he has made an elaborate show of pursuing.' But by the end of World War One the women could play a bit. The Portsmouth *Football Mail* claimed that Pioneer Ladies captain Ada Anscombe was 'the finest woman player in the country', and alleged that a male team once offered two of their men for her. The FA wouldn't have approved.

The wartime games were usually for charity, and the ladies who played a team of convalescing Canadian soldiers at Elm Park in September 1917 had already handed over £161 to various charities that year. Unfortunately, on this Wednesday afternoon, the conditions were vile. The receipts were probably swallowed up by expenses.

After a band from Bearwood Hospital had played, Surgeon-General Foster, director of the Canadian Medical Services, kicked off. The referee was Colonel Mayus, director of bayonet fighting and physical training. No decisions were disputed.

The women won 8–5 with goals from Miss Barrell (3), Miss Small (2), Miss Wragg (2) and Miss Bentley. It was suspected that the Canadian soldiers were too gallant to win, and in any event there must have been great amusement at the sight of them playing with hands behind their backs. Whether this rule was introduced to balance the sides or to make the women feel safer, I do not know.

SOCCER IN GAS MASKS

VARIOUS LOCATIONS, 1917–18

The Royal Engineers have a rich soccer heritage, so it isn't surprising to discover their participation in gas-mask soccer during World War One.

During the first seven years of the FA Cup (1871–8), the Royal Engineers faced 32 Cup-ties, winning the trophy once and reaching the FA Cup Final on three other occasions. They appeared in the first-ever FA Cup Final (1872) and might have done better than a 1–0 defeat had full-back Lieutenant Cresswell not broken his collarbone after ten minutes.

A Royal Engineers team also won the FA Amateur Cup in 1908, and memories of this success were very clear when World War One broke out. The gas-mask games became a regular part of their training towards the end of the war.

When the whistle went for the kick-off, each player had to take out his gas mask and fit it properly. He wasn't allowed to touch the ball until his mask was properly secured.

During the game the referee would stop the game by whistle and order gas masks to be removed. This time the masks had to be properly put away before players were allowed to touch the ball. The aim, of course, was to familiarize the Royal Engineers with the dexterity needed to use gas masks. The players wore full army uniform during these games, and officers hoped for no serious injuries.

If the notion of soldiers sustaining injuries in soccer games rather than war combat sounds ironic, consider the case of Eddie Mason, a member of the Dragoon Guards for seven years. Mason fought at Marne, Ypres and Aisne and survived the bloodiest war in history with hardly a scratch. Then, in 1919, playing his first game for Hull City, he was carried off in the first few minutes and missed the whole season.

TRIUMPH OF THE 'FAIR LEATHER BOOTERS'

NEW BEDFORD (MASS.), OCTOBER 1922

During the inter-war period, Dick-Kerr's factory team from Preston was the Huddersfield Town and Arsenal of women's soccer. The team toured Britain, Europe and the United States, playing in aid of charity and winning almost all their games. In their heyday, Dick-Kerr's would attract five-figure attendances. They once packed over 50,000 into Goodison Park (with many more left in the streets outside) and one game in Paris was abandoned five minutes from the end after spectators had burst on to the field to protest about a corner-kick decision.

Dick-Kerr's were a team to get excited about. Unless, of course, you happened to be a council member of the men's FA. In 1921, a consultative committee of the council claimed that women's teams were showbiz outfits exploiting football and not always devoting sufficient funds to charity. The FA therefore banned women's soccer from major football stadiums.

Fortunately, as often happens, such restrictions led to greater innovation. Take, for example, the novel 1924 floodlit match when Dick-Kerr's played Bradford Ladies and the lights were so bright it was claimed you could read the match programme in the centre of the field; or the 1922 tour of the United States, when the girls from Preston received star billing for games against a dozen American teams.

50

What an attraction Dick-Kerr's were that 1921–2 season. They turned up for matches (sometimes two a week) clad in frills and furbelows, carrying cases and parcels which contained all the essential gear – boots, shinpads, powder puffs, hairpins, etc. The team's playing kit was black-and-white striped shirts, black or blue knickers (the pre-war name for shorts) and black-and-white knitted hats. Some players, opting to play bareheaded, pinned their hair into bobs.

And what a team they were. They had a French international goalkeeper, Carmen Pomies, who had been a champion javelin-thrower before she came across the Channel to work at the Dick-Kerr's factory (now the General Electric Company). There was a consistent defence, with players such as Lily Lee and Alice Kell, both of whom were to play for years. And, most dramatically, there was a forward-line which was averaging around six goals a game. The star centre-forward, Florrie Radford, scored prolifically (about two a game); and, as in all great teams of the era, there were two entertaining wingers, Jenny Harris and Lily Parr. If Arsenal's Cliff Bastin could be dubbed 'Boy' Bastin in recognition of his early achievements, then Lily deserved to be 'Girl' Parr. After celebrating her winning goal against St Helens' Ladies at Wrexham by turning a gymnastic catherine-wheel (much to the crowd's amusement), there were typical letters to the local newspaper suggesting it was time Wrexham gave her a chance in Division Three (North).

It was from this atmosphere of adulation and heroine-worship that the girls (all unmarried and most in their very early twenties) set sail for the United States. They were on the same ship as French boxer Georges Carpentier, heavyweight and light-heavyweight champion of Europe. The girls thought Carpentier gorgeous, but they were lucky not to see him a week after his arrival in the United States, by when he had been pulped and knocked out.

The girls, meanwhile, concentrated on the more gentle pastime of soccer. They set their standards in the first minute of the tour when, playing against the men of Paterson, Alice

Woods brought down McGuire, described as a 'noted one-armed forward from Brooklyn'. Dick-Kerr's lost that game 6–3 in front of 5,000 people.

The New Bedford game was the fifth of the tour. Two had been drawn and two lost. Pre-match preparation included a sing-song in the YWCA where they were staying. The two wingers played their mouth-organs, but there was to be no more play for Lily Parr that week. She had damaged a knee playing basketball and would miss the big soccer game.

The promoters of the game had guaranteed £1,000 so they were all smiles when the biggest soccer crowd in New Bedford history turned out to see the women of England take on the local all-male team. Despite a hefty police presence (twelve men), there was little chance that passions would erupt.

Dick-Kerr's were twice behind early in the game. Each time Molly Walker equalized. Then Florrie Radford chipped in with two goals, and the women led 4–2.

Late in the game, the men pressed hard. They pulled back a goal. Then another. The scores were level with time running out. Then, in the dying minutes, Florrie Radford took a penalty-kick. Her shot was saved. No matter. A minute later Jenny Harris, the smallest player on the field, scored for the women, and they won 5–4.

There were some indications that the men had played within themselves, and that the second half had gone on a long time, but there was no disputing the final result. The Preston women, described in the American press as 'the fair leather booters', had beaten the American men.

WILFRED MINTER'S GOALSCORING FEAT

DULWICH, NOVEMBER 1922

Never has one man made such a strange goal-scoring impact on a game than Wilfred Minter did that dark Wednesday afternoon in Dulwich. The occasion was an FA Cup replay in the fourth round of the qualifying stage of the competition. In the original game, the previous Saturday, St Albans City and Dulwich Hamlet had drawn 1-1 in controversial circumstances. There was major debate as to whether Redvers Miller's corner-kick had touched any other player before it entered the net – not until 1924 were goals direct from corner-kicks permitted – but referee Rolfe decided it had and St Albans had their late equalizer.

Wilf Minter had been St Albans's outstanding forward in the first game between these two teams of amateurs. He was a local lad, having attended the Hatfield Road school and received football tuition from J. Dickinson, a former St Albans City captain. Minter entered the army when war broke out. While serving overseas he developed his fitness and football talents, and, after demobilization, played for his school old boys' team, helping them to win the 1919–20 Aubrey Cup competition. He joined St Albans City in February 1921 and soon became a goal-scoring phenomenon for club and county. Representative honours followed, but he turned down professional offers to enter his father's business and remain as an amateur with St Albans.

He was to create a record which no professional has ever matched.

The game was played at Champion Hill, Dulwich, where both the home team and St Albans were forced to field deputy goalkeepers after injuries on the Saturday. No doubt this contributed to the afternoon's entertainment. Alf Fearn, a half-back from St Albans Gasworks, was never likely to be a genius at handling corner-kicks and crosses.

Inside 15 minutes Dulwich were a goal ahead. Then Wilf Minter took over. He scored from a crossbar rebound, headed in a Pierce centre and added a third after exchanging passes with H.S. Miller.

After half an hour the score was clear-cut: Dulwich 1 (Kail), St Albans 3 (Minter 3).

During the next half-hour Alf Fearn's lack of goalkeeping experience was exposed. Dulwich scored four times.

After 60 minutes, therefore, the score conveyed a different message: Dulwich Hamlet 5 (Davis 3, Kail 2), St Albans City 3 (Minter 3).

All over? Not quite. When Harold Figg's shot hit a goal-post, Minter followed up to pull back a goal, then he shot two more to give St Albans the lead.

Seventy minutes played, and again the score was transformed: Dulwich Hamlet 5 (Davis 3, Kail 2), St Albans City 6 (Minter 6).

In these earlier days of soccer, people would dispute what was a real hat trick. To conform with the cricketing model – three wickets in three *consecutive* balls – soccer goals really needed to be three in a row rather than three in a game. But here there was no dispute. Minter had done it twice in one game – three in a row in 12 first-half minutes and three in a row again in 10 second-half minutes. Astonishing.

And there was more to come. Five minutes from the end Dulwich put the ball in the St Albans net. The referee reversed his original decision and gave a goal, much to the dismay of the St Albans players. It meant the scores were level at 6–6 after 90 minutes. Extra-time of 15 minutes each way began in fading light.

After 100 minutes Kail sprinted from the halfway-line and gave Dulwich Hamlet a 7–6 lead. In the gathering gloom, at the other end, Minter was tackled clumsily in the penalty area. Appeals for a penalty were turned down. Too dark for the referee to see, some argued.

With just four minutes to play Redvers Miller took a corner-kick for St Albans City. This time there was no doubt that someone touched the ball before it hit the net – Wilfred Minter.

Imagine the mood of the man now. Seven goals each and he has scored all his team's goals. The referee is set to blow his whistle as the 120 minutes are just about played. Then the linesman flags and the referee awards a dubious free-kick to Dulwich. Over comes the cross, Davis heads a goal for the London side. The game ends.

Dulwich Hamlet 8 (Davis 4, Kail 3, Nicol), St Albans City 7 (Minter 7).

For an individual to score seven goals is not all that uncommon, but to score *all* his team's goals including *two* hat tricks, and for the *losing* team – that was unique. The next Saturday Wilfred Minter was made captain and the band played 'For he's a jolly good fellow' when he went to the centre of the field for the coin-tossing ritual.

Whether it would have been better to win 1–0 than lose 8–7, we will leave for the modern-day managers to discuss.

EXPERIMENTING WITH THE RULES

LONDON, JANUARY 1925

The Football Association sensed that the offside law needed a radical overhaul. Ivan Sharpe, writing in *Forty Years in Football*, credits, or perhaps discredits, Morley and Montgomery, Notts County full-backs before World War One, with the invention of the offside tactic. Bill McCracken, Newcastle United's Irish international full-back, took the idea and developed it further. In McCracken's heyday, the later 1900s and early 1910s, the offside law demanded *three* players goalside of the attacker. Two full-backs with strategic minds, like McCracken and Frank Hudspeth, would combine to catch out players. As McCracken described it much later, it was putting players offside rather than waiting for them to get offside.

When Newcastle played Notts County the game would be wedged in a 20-yard section in the middle of the pitch with both teams hoping to spring the offside traps. Soon other teams caught on to the defensive tactics. Free-kicks became plentiful, scoring more difficult, and entertainment was not the same. It was generally agreed that something should be done to make the offside law fairer to forwards.

On 25 January 1925, the Football Association took advantage of the fact that several clubs, knocked out of the FA Cup, had a blank Saturday. Several experimental games were organized.

The game at Highbury, a friendly between Arsenal and

Chelsea, captured the spirit of the experiments. In the first half a line was drawn 40 yards from each goal, limiting the area in which players could be offside. In the second half the referee enforced a rule reducing the number of defenders needed between the player of the ball and the goal from three to two. There was only one offside decision in the whole game – there was only one goal too (scored by Chelsea) – and referee Mr Todman (from Croydon) found it a pleasure not needing to blow his whistle so much. He preferred the two-man plan to the 40-yards idea. The general conclusion was that the experiment was worth a try in a more competitive setting.

There were several other trial games that day – at Clapton (against Wolves), at Charlton (against Luton), at Norwich (against Cambridge University) and an amateur game between the West Riding and Staffordshire, where the 40-yard line was deemed a success and one observer wondered whether the halfway-line marking was now needed, except for the bit in the centre-circle.

Perhaps the most pertinent comments were those of Mr Pilch, the referee at Norwich, who was quoted in the *Athletic News*: 'If two defenders, instead of three, govern the operation of the offside law, football will faster and a tremendous amount more interesting. I feel absolutely confident that the suggested alteration will make the game much more interesting for spectators. We must take things as they are, not as we would like them to be.'

After a few more experimental matches during the remainder of the season, the two-man plan was adopted by the Football Association in time for the 1925–6 season.

STRIKERS AGAINST POLICE

PLYMOUTH, MAY 1926

It seems strange that striking trade-unionists would play the police at soccer on the day of their most intense conflict in history, yet such a match occurred in Plymouth during the 1926 General Strike. A crowd of over 10,000 saw the strikers win by two goals to one. The policemen had their work cut out – on and off the field.

Industrial unrest among northern coal-miners had spread to other industries and services. The effects reached Plymouth later than most towns, but the outcome was devastating. At the end of the first week in May the General Strike was a week old, and the *Western Morning News and Mercury* was talking of a state bordering on Civil War: 'Football is all very well in normal circumstances, and there is no reason why policemen and workmen should not play it. But conditions today are not normal, and a match between policemen and strikers is, at least, strange.'

The events of the Saturday confirmed some people's worst fears. Tramway employers tempted fate by resuming a modified service using volunteers and inspectors to replace the 800 workers who were on strike. Confrontation and chaos was the result. During the morning crowds gathered in the town-centre to prevent tramcars passing.

By 11.30 that Saturday morning there were around 4,000 people doing their best to block the trams. Amidst the jostling a few stones smashed tramcar windows. About 20 or 30 policemen charged the crowd, wielding batons, but it did not prevent the continued harassment of the tramcars. Ironically, this happened just before the soccer match was due to start at Home Park. Once again the police and the strikers were on opposite sides.

The tramway team scored midway through the first half, and a wave of enthusiasm greeted this first – dare I say it? – strike.

Another ironic touch came at half-time, when the music was provided by the tramway band – workers at the very heart of the dispute. When the second-half started, large sections of the crowd followed the band off the pitch and out of the stadium. By the time the strikers scored their second goal, ten minutes from the end, the tramway band was leading a procession of people, four by four, walking along the tramlines to ensure no cars passed. There were more ugly scenes.

Mounted police were called in to deal with a 20,000 crowd in Old Town Street. Three arrests were made, but the tramcar service was withdrawn and the likelihood of pitched battle averted. The next week the strike was called off, leaving the Plymouth strikers with a 100 per cent record on the soccer pitch. That same month games also took place between the Sheffield Police and strikers at Park Colliery.

AMATEURS VERSUS PROFESSIONALS

MANCHESTER, OCTOBER 1926

Take a team of professionals, familiar with each other's play. Include five England internationals. Then pick a team of assorted amateur players. Now play the amateurs against the professionals. Who would win? Yes, the amateurs, of course.

On five occasions, during the 1920s, the Professionals played the Amateurs for the FA Charity Shield. It was soccer's equivalent of the Gentlemen-Players cricket match. There were some who said the professionals played these midweek games with their minds on the week-end Football League programme, but there was certainly pride at stake. In the 1926 Professionals' team there were internationals such as Tom Magee (West Brom), David Jack (Bolton), Bill Rawlings (Southampton), Joe Smith (Bolton) and Fred Tunstall (Sheffield United). The team was selected from the FA party which had toured Canada the previous close-season.

The Professionals scored three goals that afternoon at Maine Road, Manchester, but in between Rawlings's second in the 30th minute and Tunstall's in the last the Amateurs hit half a dozen. Edgar Kail, a full international before the end of the decade, scored the first. Wilfred Minter scored the second. Macey hit the next two, the second from 25 yards, Minter got another, and the sixth was an own-goal. The Amateurs won 6–3.

INTRODUCING THE EIGHT-SQUARE GAME

LONDON, JANUARY 1927

Broadcasting was in its infancy. The idea of putting a soccer match on the BBC and relaying news through the wireless system throughout Britain was original, exciting and challenging. The game chosen for the experiment was Arsenal against Sheffield United, two teams in the middle of Division One. There was nothing special about the game, just that it could capture the attention of people outside Highbury Stadium.

That week the *Radio Times* carried a front-page plan of the Highbury pitch, dividing it into eight equal sections. Each section was numbered for easy identification. Low numbers (one to four) indicated a team's own half of the field, high numbers (five to eight) that it had possession in the opposition half. Odd numbers referred to the left side of the team, even numbers meant the right. The sections were called 'squares', but if they were genuine squares, Highbury must have had a different-shaped pitch that day.

Two commentators were used. Mr Wakelam described the play, and, in the background, Mr Lewis called out the square numbers. This informed the audience who had the ball and exactly where play was occurring. They could sit with the *Radio Times* plan in front of them and follow the verbal action.

This experiment, following closely after the broadcasting of the England-Wales rugby international, was considered a

61

success, though there were some criticisms in newspapers, as might perhaps be expected from a rival reporting network. Some said the account was disconnected, delivered too rapidly or that several players were wrongly identified by the commentators. Well, it was early days.

Appropriately, the first two goals scored on radio, knocked in from squares seven and eight, went to two of the biggest names in soccer at the time – England international Charlie Buchan (Arsenal) and Ireland international Billy Gillespie (Sheffield United). The game finished 1–1.

Soccer broadcasting expanded rapidly. Ten million people, it was estimated, listened to the regular BBC broadcasts of Arsenal director George Allison (commentator) and Derek 'Uncle Mac' McCulloch (square caller), and three months after the Highbury game the FA Cup Final was broadcasted. Soccer was on its way to a new era. Local celebrities would become national heroes. Ordinary supporters, accustomed to reading about their team and chatting to one another, would suddenly discover how a player's name sounded with a BBC accent. Blind people would have their interest in soccer resurrected. And commentators learned the power of information.

EIGHT ON A DEBUT

STIRLING, JANUARY 1930

When a strange result occurs, there is usually a set of logical explanations. Take this match, for instance. Why would King's Park, a Scottish Second Division team, beat Forfar Athletic, a team above them in the division, by the ridiculous score of 12–2?

There were four main reasons. First there was the Forthbank pitch, greasy in places, ankle-deep almost everywhere, the sort of clinging, cloying pitch that saps the energy of opponents once a home team gets a substantial lead. Second, there was the Forfar defence, which was missing four regular players. Third, there was the King's Park attack, which included a newcomer called John Dyet, who was on trial at centre-forward. Fourth, there was the date, Thursday 2 January, the day after a full league programme of soccer games, shortly after the celebrations of New Year's Eve.

Perhaps the most dramatic factor was the introduction of Dyet, who replaced Martin, injured in the 3–2 defeat at East Stirling the day before, at centre-forward. Dyet, a Cowie juvenile player, brother of King's Park left-half Gilbert, scored six goals in the first half. At the interval the home team led 7–0, Duffy having scored the third of the seven.

Forfar, who had won 4–3 against Arbroath on New Year's Day, included their own star forward, Davie Kilgour, the Second Division top scorer with 24 goals. Kilgour, likely

63

to be overtaken in two games if Dyet kept up his first-half pace, pulled back a goal with a penalty shortly after half-time.

King's Park added a further three goals, scored by Ross, Baird and Duffy, before Forfar scored again. Then Dyet chipped in with two more goals before the end.

King's Park wasted no time in signing the youngster. Eight goals and a record score seemed as much as could be expected from Dyet on his debut. Besides, there were clubs queuing up outside the Forthbank stadium, just in case he slipped through the net that afternoon.

King's Park ended the season one point above Forfar Athletic in the league table.

EXPOSING CHELSEA'S DEFENCE

BLACKPOOL, OCTOBER 1931

Footballers are soft these days, old-time players are fond of telling us. They play in 'carpet slippers', use balloons as footballs and have games postponed if there's a spot of rain on the pitch. An exaggeration, perhaps, but the old-timers could point to plenty of evidence when Chelsea took a fateful trip to the seaside in October, 1931. The game at Blackpool was more a question of how many players would collapse with hypothermia and exposure. At full-time Chelsea were left with six men.

It was a cold, miserable, windy day with ferocious driving rain. Fifteen minutes before kick-off the Bloomfield Road stadium was comparatively deserted. The eventual gathering of 6,000 spectators was about half the usual size. It was a wonder the game started, and Chelsea later complained that the pitch was unfit. Ground staff worked with pitchforks in a futile attempt to clear the water.

Chelsea, missing their famous Scottish International Hughie Gallacher (how glad he must have been), won the toss and sensibly opted to kick with the wind behind them. But conditions soon proved almost impossible. The ball either plopped in mud or squirted over grease. The first chance fell to Jimmy Hampson of Blackpool but he lost the ball in one of the more shallow lakes.

Chelsea found it hopeless to pursue their normal short-passing game and soon trailed to Wilkinson's 12th-minute goal. Even the referee had difficulty. Mr Jones of Nottingham lost his balance and tumbled to his knees, much to the amusement of the spectators.

In the 31st and 34th minutes Jimmy Hampson scored two freak goals to give Blackpool a 3–0 half-time lead. First the England international centre-forward dribbled round Vic Woodley as the Chelsea goalkeeper lost his footing in the mud. Then Woodley stooped to intercept a cross, fell on both knees, and gasped in amazement as the ball stopped dead in the mud a yard from him. Hampson stepped in, used his foot as a spade and thanked the weather for his second goal.

At half-time came the first sensation. Peter O'Dowd, soon to become England's centre-half, slumped unconscious in the dressing-room. His body temperature had dropped dangerously low. Two other Chelsea players were overcome by the cold. The second half started with only eight in the Chelsea team. Although they were soon restored to ten men, nobody relished the water-polo activities in the Chelsea penalty area. Blackpool's long-ball game was well-suited to the conditions and Hampson completed his hat-trick in the 75th minute.

Immediately after Blackpool's fourth goal, two Chelsea players left the field. The crowd booed and jeered, but it didn't stop another Chelsea player limping off. Soon there were only six left. And, on the same day (31 October), at nearby Blackburn, two of the home side and three Sheffield United players were treated for exposure, while the referee collapsed from the cold. After a 20-minute delay, a linesman completed the game.

At the end of that season (1931–2), Blackpool escaped relegation from the First Division by one point. They were grateful to the day at Bloomfield Road when Chelsea's defence was exposed to the cold.

But even in the 1930s some old-timers were doubtless arguing that it was tougher in their day. There was a famous occasion at Grimsby (in 1912) when six Leicester Fosse players walked off the pitch ten minutes from the end of their 4–0 defeat, and Leicester trainer Harley Thompson was later suspended for enticing them off. And Ernest Needham, Sheffield United's famous international at the turn of the century, recalled a numbing experience at Aston Villa. Writing in his book *Association Football*, he described it like this: 'The bitterly cold wind and sleet pierced one, numbing muscle and brain. Men on both sides succumbed and were carried away to hot baths and stimulants. I left the field half an hour before the finish of time, and by so doing probably saved my life. Even Foulke was carried in completely exhausted. Several of the Villans did what playing they could in great coats, and one used an umbrella.'

THE FASTEST INDIVIDUAL GOALS

WEST HAM, NOVEMBER 1931

Picture yourself as a supporter of a team which hasn't won for four games. (Some will find this easier than others.) Your centre-forward, Richardson, hasn't been playing well. You would prefer Cookson in Richardson's place at centre-forward. Now you have an away game against a team in London, which means a difficult journey of over 100 miles. However, as the London team is not playing well, you think your side has a chance. You decide to go, but have difficulty finding the ground – your team was promoted to the First Division at the end of last season – and arrive late. You make your way on to the terraces and see someone you know.

'How are we doing?' you ask your mate, knowing that you have missed about ten minutes of the game.

'We're four-nil up,' he replies casually. 'Richardson's got all four and he should have had two more.'

Would you believe him?

Yet, that day in November 1931, you would have had to. W.G.Richardson, the West Bromwich Albion centre-forward, had two good chances in the first five minutes and missed them. Then he scored four times in the next five minutes. It was a remarkable spell of sustained rapid goalscoring, taking advantage of some weak West Ham full-back play and the fact that England international centre-half Jim Barrett was playing out of position at left-half.

The game was virtually over as a contest almost as soon as it had begun. The next goal, scored just after the hour, by Sandford, put West Brom five goals ahead. Jimmy Ruffell headed a reply soon afterwards, and West Ham went down 5–1 on their own ground.

W.G.Richardson's four goals in five minutes is the quickest scoring of four goals on record, a feat equalling that of Jimmy McIntyre of Blackburn Rovers a decade earlier. The difference was that McIntyre's goals came in the second half. Richardson set off one of the quickest starts a soccer game has known.

THE LIFE OR DEATH GAME

NEWARK, NOVEMBER 1931

Keeping a football club alive during the early years of a major economic depression was not an easy business. Halifax Town of Division Three (North) found it more difficult than most. At the start of the 1929–30 season, when wages were owed to players, the club was reported to the Football Association. Directors resigned, creditors sued and the club tottered from week to week until the end of the season, when they were re-elected.

Halifax Town survived the first years of the 1930s through loans, donations, an SOS appeal ('Soccer on Shay') and the sale of players, like Ernest Dixon (to Huddersfield Town), Cliff Binns (Blackburn Rovers) and Sedley Cooper (Sheffield Wednesday). Another economic ally was the FA Cup, which offered the hope of good attendances in later rounds.

The 1931–2 FA Cup competition started with Halifax drawn away to Newark Town in the first round. It was a game Halifax couldn't afford to lose. The club's dire financial position meant that defeat could be the end of Halifax Town's history.

The tension at Newark that day was extreme. The atmosphere was alive with anxiety. The Halifax players knew that the future of the club rested on the game against Newark, and their concern increased when Newark took the lead within a few minutes of the start. Nor did Halifax play well when Newark lost a player with injury. Fortunately, by half-time

Halifax had levelled the scores, the goal being scored by Mays, who had played for Wales while with Wrexham.

The tale of the second half is best told by T.T.Dickinson, who wrote the 1937 *History & Records of Halifax Town AFC*: 'One of the tensest struggles I have ever seen followed. Town had to defend as if for dear life – they simply dare not lose – while Newark attacked like furies. In the last 15 minutes the suspense was almost unbearable, and when someone handed a cigarette to Benny Wheelhouse, who, unfit, was watching the game from the touchline, he chewed it up and ate it in his excitement. Dick Strang, at centre halfback, was a hero for Halifax Town on that never-to-be-forgotten day.'

Halifax hung on to draw 1–1, beat Newark 2–1 at home, overcame Accrington 3–0 in the second round and lost to Bournemouth in the third round. Four sets of receipts rather than one. Halifax Town lived on. Next season (1932–3) they were even more grateful for FA Cup receipts. Halifax reached the fifth round (last 16) and played a strange cup-tie with Luton Town, losing 2–0. The Halifax captain was never forgiven for playing against the wind in the first half. It began to snow and a blizzard swept so strongly into the faces of Halifax defenders that the game was stopped for 20 minutes.

SIX IN TWENTY-ONE MINUTES

LINCOLN, JANUARY 1932

Lincoln City were at home to Halifax Town. Lincoln had completed more than half of their Division Three (North) fixtures for the season and only one team had stopped them scoring in a game – Halifax Town. The game at the Shay had finished 3–0 to the home team.

Lincoln, with the wind behind them, scored twice during the first half of the return but play was fairly even. The goals came from Riley and Hall, the latter being in the middle of an exceptionally good run. 'I hav sung of Alan Hall, whos a terrer with the ball,' wrote a rhymer who specialized in the local vernacular.

The goal blitz started in the 46th minute. Lincoln scored seven in 21 minutes, and, strangely, Hall was not among the second-half scorers. Frank Keetley scored six. Wrote our rhymer friend, 'I hav toled of how Frank Keetley, shoots so well and passes needly.'

Keetley, who had missed the previous game due to injury, took advantage of the extra marking on Hall to steer Lincoln to their 9–1 win. Lincoln went to the top of Division Three (North) and that season they won the championship on goal average. Alan Hall scored 42 League goals – he is still Lincoln's highest scorer in a season – but the home game against Halifax was Frank Keetley's day.

THE GAME WITH TWO REFEREES

CHESTER, JANUARY 1935

Two referees and two linesmen. The idea came from the Referees' Committee. The game chosen for experiment was an England Amateur international trial between teams from the North and South. It was a bad choice. The amateurs were so well-behaved that nothing was tested. One clear-cut penalty was awarded, converted by Simms in the North's 3–1 win, but, otherwise, there were barely enough decisions for one referee, let alone two.

The referees at Chester were Dr A.W.Barton, a Repton schoolmaster from Derby, and Mr E.Wood of Sheffield. Early in the game they were tempted across the halfway-line a few times before they realized their more limited responsibilities. Onlookers wondered what would happen if an incident occurred in one referee's half and the other was in a better position to judge. Who would decide then?

A second attempt was made later that season. The same two referees, Barton and Wood, were given control of a professional international trial, England against the Rest. Again the outcome was inconclusive as there was not enough work for two men. The Football Association might have learned more from a competition where the referees were stretched, perhaps at local-league level, rather than the games at Chester and West Bromwich.

Observers' reactions were generally negative. The idea never caught on, the detail was never worked out. The spectators would have needed to distinguish between the two referees (red whistle and yellow whistle?) to know whom to insult. Yet, had the idea been instigated, we might today have players voting in the dressing-rooms and sponsors offering a prize – Referee of the Match.

'AVALANCHE AT ASTON'

ASTON, DECEMBER 1935

Before the away game at bottom-of-the-league Aston Villa, Arsenal centre-forward Ted Drake was worried because he hadn't been scoring too well. He contacted his manager, George Allison, who was in hospital at the time. Allison wrote back indicating how he felt Arsenal could get a 'sackful' of goals against Villa.

On paper it was not an easy fixture. Although Villa were bottom of the First Division, they had spent a lot of money signing new players. Their new team contained six internationals, and it seemed only a matter of time before they put together some good results.

The crowd must have formed the same impression during the first 20 minutes of the game against Arsenal. Villa did most of the attacking but couldn't score. Then Arsenal broke away and Ted Drake scored with his first shot. He also scored with his second, third, fourth, fifth and sixth shots. He hit the crossbar with his seventh, then slammed in his seventh goal with his eighth attempt of the day. Arsenal won 7–1, Palethorpe scoring for Villa shortly after Drake had notched his second hat-trick.

Drake, in fact, scored a hat-trick in each half. His fifth and sixth goals were struck with the supreme confidence of a man who just could not miss the target. Villa had their chances – Palethorpe nearly made it 1–1 with a header and had the ball in the net at 3–0 only to discover Arsenal had been

75

given a free-kick – but the difference between the teams lay in Drake's finishing.

Ted Drake, a £6,000 signing from Southampton, was still in his early 20s. The next year he scored Arsenal's cup-winning goal at Wembley and he helped them to two League Championships. He won five England caps and, as a manager, took Chelsea to the League Championship in 1954–5. Altogether, it was a remarkable career, although he is remembered by many for that sensational day at Villa Park when he earned headlines such as DRAKE'S ARMADA and AVALANCHE AT ASTON.

TEN GOALS AT HIS FIRST ATTEMPT

LUTON, APRIL 1936

Easter Monday at Kenilworth Road. The home team, Luton Town, preparing for a Third Division (South) game against Bristol Rovers, discovered that they had two centre-forwards on the injury-list. Manager Ned Liddell opted for Joe Payne as a replacement. Payne, a reserve wing-half, had some experience of playing in the forward-line but had never appeared there in the Luton first team. Yet Payne made such an impact that his record may never be beaten.

There was no early hint of what was to come. Payne collected a goal in the 23rd minute and Roberts soon made it 2–0 to Luton, but, five minutes before half-time, the game could have gone either way. Then Joe Payne scored nine in 46 minutes, and no one else scored during this incredible period. With three headers and seven shots, Joe Payne had scored ten goals on his first attempt at centre-forward. Martin scored one in the last minute to make the final score 12–0.

The previous individual scoring record was nine, and Joe Payne's record of ten in a Football League game has held ever since. Payne, a former Derbyshire coal-miner, was 22 years old at the time of his baptism at centre-forward. Two years later, in 1938, he went to Chelsea for £2,000, already an England international. During the war he twice broke an ankle, and never added to the one cap he won against Finland, when he scored two goals. After the war he scored six League goals for West Ham in a spell of nine months – four goals less than he managed in 63 minutes that sensational day at Luton.

TAKING IT AT WALKING PACE

DERBY, MAY 1937

This was the sixth annual walking match between the Crewe and Derby Railway Veterans Associations. Derby held the Cup, having won 2–0 at Crewe in 1936, and were looking to win it two years running (not that the referee would have allowed that).

All the players were over 65 years old. The oldest, Young (Derby) and Betley (Crewe), were both 73. The venue was the Baseball Ground, home of Derby County, and 1,500 spectators turned out on a fine day. The game was one of the most bizarre ever refereed by Arthur Kingscott, who had officiated in two FA Cup Finals, but he had no difficulty keeping up with play, which, at times, reached the frenzied pace of six miles per hour.

Crewe started well on top and looked set for a walkaway victory. By comparison Derby looked pedestrian, which, of course, they were. But once Derby discovered their wing men, the pattern of play changed. Their left-wing pair of Collier and Briddon walked rings round the Crewe right flank, while Radford, only 67, put in some good walks and centres on the Derby right. Radford had the best chance of the match, only the goalkeeper to beat, but shot five yards wide. The crowd groaned. They felt he could have walked the ball in.

The build-up of both teams was slow, naturally, but there was no holding back by the players. One or two of them

79

received minor knocks but were advised by the trainer to 'walk it off'. There were only two things missing. The occasion deserved a walking commentary from a radio station and it also needed a goal.

The game ended 0–0 and both teams shared the Cup, which was filled to the brim and passed round the players at the end. Crewe were optimistic about their chances the next season, when they would be at home. They had a younger team than Derby – average age 68 as against Derby's 69 – and knew the Derby 'lads' would be a year older when they met again.

A MATTER OF CLASS

ETON, DECEMBER 1938

In December 1938 the playing fields of Eton College staged one of the strangest games of Britain's class-conscious society. The Eton College school team took on St Helen's Auckland Social Service team, which was mainly comprised of unemployed coal-miners from the north-east.

Two years previously, Eton College had 'adopted' the St Helen's Social Club centre as part of a goodwill exercise during the days of severe economic depression. Periodically, the boys and staff of the College had travelled to the Durham village of Auckland, involving themselves in the local community activities. As the *Auckland Chronicle* put it, 'Taking part in the sing-songs, the village teas and suppers, and dances gave them an insight into that quality of warm hospitality which is the quality of the north.'

Now came the opportunity for a trip of a lifetime. The Auckland boys were invited to visit the College at the expense of the Etonians. A game of football was part of the excursion. The tough, gritty northern lads were expected to give the Eton schoolboys a pretty good game.

At 8 am on Wednesday 14 December, a party of 18 Auckland boys and seven officials set off by motor-coach on the 250-mile journey south. They were cheered loudly by mothers, sisters and sweethearts, who had gathered on a chilly morning to give them a good send-off to the 'far distant land'.

81

Only six of the party travelling south were in employment. The rest were wondering where their next wage would come from. But for one day the young men from the north-east were given the chance to live like the 1,160 boys at Eton College. On arrival, they were given a hot supper and hotel accommodation. 'They are champion,' one north-easterner said of his southern hosts. 'It's like home from home.'

In the morning the north-east party breakfasted with the schoolboys and attended the Chapel service. Later, after watching work begin in the classrooms, they were taken to see Windsor Castle and St George's Chapel. Then they toured the College buildings and were shown the Tuck Shop – a strategic move, as the football game started shortly afterwards.

The Auckland lads were surprised by the quality of the Eton schoolboys' play. The contest between the polished students and the rough-and-ready unemployed coal-miners was an even one. The result was a 2–2 draw.

The boys ate tea in the College Hall and stayed a second night before travelling home the next day. They agreed that the trip had been grand. One of them, centre-half Makinson, spoke of the best three days of his life.

'THE MOST FREAKISH, GOALFUL REPRESENTATIVE MATCH OF ALL TIME'

LIVERPOOL, APRIL 1941

'The most freakish, goalful representative match of all time,' wrote L.E.E. of the *Liverpool Daily Post*. 'It will become one of the talked-of "classics" even if, on this occasion, there was no rabid club partisanship to fire enthusiasms.'

In one respect the reporter was correct – it was the most amazing representative match of all time. In another respect he was sadly wrong – the game between the Football League and a British XI, in aid of the Lord Mayor's Fund, hasn't been mentioned much since that day in April 1941.

Freakishness was quite common during wartime games. Teams were often selected at the last minute because players' availability was in doubt. There are countless examples of double-figure scores being registered against variegated teams containing something like half a dozen assorted professionals, a couple of out-of-position reserves, a cocky local just out of the pub, a spectator who falsely claimed to have played for Aldershot and a trainer playing his first game since Wembley was built.

But this game wasn't like that. The players were all stars. More than half were internationals, nine had played in FA Cup Finals, and there wasn't a laggard amongst them, although there were several decidedly strange incidents.

83

One of these was the injury of Alf Hobson, the Chester and ex-Liverpool goalkeeper, shortly before half-time. Playing for the Football League – and playing brilliantly – Hobson fell on his head and was carried off with concussion. Tom Galley, the Wolves wing-half, took on the goalkeeper's jersey and also played brilliantly. Billy Liddell of Liverpool joined the game as a substitute.

At half-time, the League led 3–2, but the second half brought eleven goals. Wags suggested that the cricket season had come a month early.

There is only space here to give the order of scoring: Stephenson (1–0 to the League), Nieuwenhuys (1–1), Dorsett (2–1 to the League), Cullis (2–2), Lawton (3–2 to the League), Busby (3–3), Lawton (4–3 to the League), Liddell (5–3), Fagan (5–4), Fagan (5–5), Hanson (6–5 to the League), Lawton (7–5), Stephenson own-goal (7–6), Dorsett (8–6), Stevenson (8–7) and Hanson (9–7 to the Football League).

It may be difficult to believe, but certain reporters at the game commented that it was only the goalkeepers who kept the scores down. And there is a rumour that a dour Lancastrian among the 15,000 crowd turned to his mate at the end of the game: 'Ee, lad, just think. It could easily have finished nowt-nowt.'

A Cup-tie during the 1930s depression, and not the best of weather. Supporters of Halifax Town, a club which relied on strange Cup-ties for economic survival, do their best to watch a fifth-round game against Luton Town. The blizzard caused a stoppage during the game, but only for twenty minutes.
(*Illustrated London News Picture Library*)

A men's football team once allegedly offered two players in exchange for Ada Anscombe, seen here in 1916 scoring a penalty for Portsmouth Ladies against the Postal Workers. That same season a Portsmouth women's munitions team took on a team of Canadian men who played with their hands behind their backs. (*Illustrated London News Picture Library*)

Eton College boys and unemployed coal-miners from West Auckland in Durham watch their teams play the game that cut across class boundaries in 1938.
(*Illustrated London News Picture Library*)

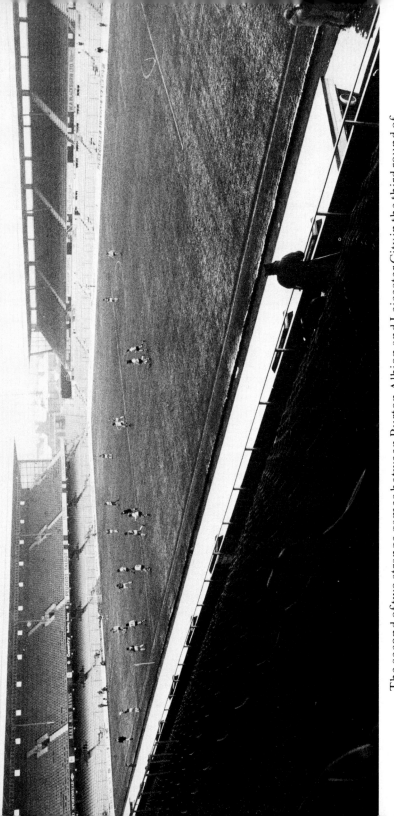

The second of two strange games between Burton Albion and Leicester City in the third round of the FA Cup in January 1985. This one was played behind closed doors at Coventry. (*Burton Mail*)

Referee Kelvin Morton awarded five penalties in a game between Crystal Palace and Brighton & Hove Albion at Easter 1989. The four shown here were all taken at the same end inside 15 minutes' play. Palace's Mark Bright scores powerfully from the first ... (*Croydon Advertiser*)

... but Bright then mis-kicks the second and Brighton's Glen Keeley saves with his legs ... (*Croydon Advertiser*)

. . . and Ian Wright puts Palace's third penalty against a
post . . . (*Croydon Advertiser*)

. . . before Alan Curbishley scores one for Brighton just after
half-time. (*Brighton Argus*)

Aston Villa's Chris Nicholl (second right) scores the third of his four goals in the 2-2 draw with Leicester City in 1976. This one was for Leicester. (*Leicester Mercury*)

A 1930 camera crew films a soccer scene for *The Great Game*, which was probably the first soccer talkie. A string of soccer movies have followed, including classics like *Escape to Victory* and *Gregory's Girl*. (*Illustrated London News Picture Library*)

Less than ten minutes gone, and W.G. Richardson's hat-trick
goal disappears past West Ham goalkeeper Ted Hufton. The
West Brom centre-forward scored another in the next minute in
the game with the fastest individual scoring.
(*Illustrated London News Picture Library*)

A simple formula for a strange game: trees as goal-posts, a path
across the pitch, some tinkering with the rules and a dog hungry
for a goal. Children play at Stourbridge, Worcestershire, as
spectators drive past. (*Andy Ward*)

Oxford City's Eales (left) celebrates his goal against Alvechurch in an FA Cup replay in 1971. Little did he realize that the two teams would have to play for eleven hours to settle the tie ...
(*Oxford Mail*)

Over 500 playing minutes later, in the sixth game, at Villa Park, Eales (right) appeals for an equalizer after Alvechurch goalkeeper Ward has pushed a header from Stokes on to the underside of the crossbar. Hunt is poised to scramble the ball away. Had the referee given a goal, the tie could easily have gone to a seventh game. At the final whistle both teams celebrated with champagne. (*Oxford Mail*)

FARCE IN THE FOG

LONDON, NOVEMBER 1945

Moscow Dynamo's four-match tour of Britain attracted considerable publicity. The third match of the tour, against Arsenal, was unanimously described as a farce. It was played in a pea-soup fog at White Hart Lane, Tottenham – Arsenal's ground was still requisitioned for war use – and contained many disputes typical of matches between British teams and Continental opposition during that era. Post-match whining shifted between the Russian referee's system and decisions, the fouling, substitutions and, of course, the weather. In one afternoon the Russians were treated to a range of love-hate emotions.

The public became aware of a culture clash at the start of Dynamo's first match of the tour, against Chelsea, when each Russian player presented a bouquet of flowers to his opposite number. They drew that game 3–3, then beat Cardiff City 10–1 to set up an intriguing fixture with Arsenal. George Allison, Arsenal manager, included six guests in his team, the most famous being Stan Matthews and Stan Mortensen (both Blackpool) and Joe Bacuzzi (Fulham).

Fog muffles sound and destroys vision, and London in the 1940s provided regular experience. There is one story about a Charlton Athletic match being abandoned and the players lying in the bath before they realized goalkeeper Sam Bartram was not among them. They found him still in his goalmouth, hopping about, staying alert, thinking his team must be doing all the attacking.

The White Hart Lane farce shouldn't have started. According to the players, visibility was down to a yard or two. The Russian referee encouraged criticism by sticking to the Russian linear system of refereeing rather than the British diagonal system. The two British linesmen were on the same side of the pitch, helped a little by their luminous flags, a novelty in Britain.

Moscow Dynamo scored in the first minute but went 3–1 behind to goals by Ronnie Rooke and Stan Mortensen (2). At half-time Arsenal led 3–2.

Arsenal made a substitution at half-time – goalkeeper Brown for goalkeeper Williams – but later complained that Dynamo had substituted a player in the fog without anybody going off. There were also complaints that players from both sides were committing fouls and then sneaking back into the fog before the referee saw them. Considering visibility was so poor, people had amazing opinions of what was happening elsewhere on the pitch, such as the complaints about the last two Dynamo goals being offside or the shirt-pulling on Stan Matthews. Dynamo won 4–3, and, after the farce was completed, people agreed that the Russians were an excellent team, the best to visit Britain, a passing combination rather than individual dribblers. They went to Glasgow and drew 2–2 with Rangers before leaving.

THE 203–MINUTE GAME

STOCKPORT, MARCH 1946

No one had yet conceived penalty-kick deciders. When the Division Three North wartime Cup-tie between Stockport County and Doncaster Rovers ended in a draw after extra-time, the two teams were asked to settle the outcome that day. The first team to score would win. But the scores were still level after 203 minutes when the game was abandoned through bad light.

The players were perhaps fortunate that the game didn't take place a month later. Had the clocks been on summer time, play might have lasted until eight o'clock.

The Cup-tie had two legs. The first, at Doncaster, ended in a 2–2 draw. The second, at Stockport, finished with the same 2–2 scoreline. The competition rules dictated extra-time of ten minutes each way. This was played with no scoring. Then the teams played on until the first goal. Referee Baker of Crewe proved a hard taskmaster.

Three times Stockport's Ken Shaw had chances to add to the two goals he had scored in the first 90 minutes. Each time the chance went astray. The game went on and on. Stockport's Les Cocker (later trainer of Leeds United and England) put the ball into the Doncaster net but Mr Baker disallowed the point for an infringement.

There were 13,000 spectators at the game and most stayed until the end. Some went home for their tea and then came back again.

The teams toiled on. The sultry heat took its toll. After 200 minutes Stockport's Rickards tried a shot in the failing light. The ball cannoned off two Doncaster defenders and the goalkeeper. All three Rovers players were left laid out like ninepins. Eventually, after 203 minutes, the referee ended the endurance test. The two teams tossed a coin for choice of ground in the replay. Rovers won the toss and chose their own ground. The following Wednesday they beat Stockport 4–0.

WHEN TWO PLAYERS DIED

ALDERSHOT, APRIL 1948

Soccer can be a lethal game. The most common causes of football death have been serious head injuries (such as those received by the much-lamented Scottish international Jock Thomson), internal injuries (for instance, William Walker of Leith in 1907), pneumonia (e.g. Sam Wynne of Bury in 1927) and infections of wounds, particularly in the earlier years of the game, when internationals like Dunlop and Di Jones died in such circumstances.

Other more unusual fatal incidents have occurred on the field. Thomas Grice of Ashton, Cheshire, fell during a game in 1897 and his belt buckle punctured his stomach. A game in Alicante, Spain, in 1924 was interrupted when the ball brought down a live electric wire and a player who went to remove it was electrocuted. James Beaumont was killed at Walkley, Sheffield, in 1877 when, chasing the ball, he jumped into a quarry.

Such accidents may happen, but clubs can plan emergency procedures, medical help and safety precautions to minimize their impact. Sometimes, though, death comes too suddenly. This was the case with the Army Cup Final replay of 1948.

The Cup Finalists were the Royal Armoured Corps (Bovington) and No. 121 Training Regiment of the Royal Artillery (Oswestry). Their first meeting, on Wednesday 14 April, was a 0–0 draw distinguished only by the presence of the King and Queen. The royal schedule was delayed by half an hour because extra-time was played.

The replay also took place at the Command Central Ground in Aldershot. Oswestry scored twice in the first 20 minutes and held their lead into the second half. A storm gathered some distance away. Rain was imminent. Forked lightning flashed its warning. The players took their positions for a throw-in on the opposite side to the grandstand. There was an electric flash of lightning and a simultaneous roar of thunder. The throw-in was never taken.

It was never known what attracted the lightning – some suggested the referee's whistle, others a water-pipe around the track – but the effect was devastating. Eight players and the referee swayed from side to side and then keeled over as though they had been hit on the back of the head. Two players died in the incident – 18-year-old Bertram Boardley, the left-half of the Oswestry team, and his direct opponent, Kenneth Hill of Bovington. The referee, Captain Green, who was on the Football League list, was detained in hospital that evening, and it was suggested that wearing rubber composition footwear might have helped him survive. Two other players and two spectators were also detained in hospital.

For about 30 seconds after the incident no one seemed to have understood what had happened. Then spectators and ambulance men began to move towards the injured. But virtually everyone was in a state of shock, and spectators commented on experiencing a tingling sensation. The game was abandoned and the two teams were given the Army Cup for six months each. The verdict on the dead men was 'death by misadventure, from heart failure, due to an electric shock from lightning'.

DAYLIGHT ROBBERY

SCARBOROUGH, APRIL 1949

It is not unusual for thieves to raid a dressing-room while a game is in progress. My favourite story concerns a local game in the West Country. Two players, sent off by the referee, returned to the dressing-rooms when a robbery was taking place. They shouted the news, and all 22 players set off around the district to corner the robbers.

At Scarborough, on Easter Monday 1949, the thieves had an easier escape. The robbery took place during the first half, while Scarborough, third from bottom in the Midland League, were holding League leaders Gainsborough Trinity very creditably. The robbery was discovered at half-time. Money, wristwatches, cigarette lighters and fountain-pens were missing. The pockets of all the Scarborough players had been rifled, the referee and linesmen were victims too, and only the Gainsborough dressing-room was untouched. (Ah, Holmes, do you think this means it was a Gainsborough supporter? I think not, Watson.)

Scarborough goalkeeper Cyril Hannaby lost the key to his fish-and-chip shop in Doncaster and his return train ticket home. Bill Parke, the captain, lost his return ticket to York. Dennis Kirby lost his return ticket to Leeds. (Why, Holmes, the thieves must have split up after the robbery? Not necessarily, Watson.)

A tannoy announcement asked for Detective-Officer Bond, who was among the 3,500 crowd at the game.

There were few clues. No sign of a break-in. The thieves had probably sneaked in through the main doors and reached the dressing-room by the main passage. It was disconcerting for Scarborough players, who had the second half to play. On the field they were robbed of victory too. After taking the lead late in the game, they conceded an own-goal with the last kick of the match. Scarborough's 1–1 draw was their best performance of the season, but it was an afternoon of mixed feelings.

'FOOTBALL'S MOST AMAZING EXPERIMENT'

HINCKLEY, APRIL 1949

There is a long-running football joke about a hypnotist who is called into a team's dressing-room to improve ailing performances. The hypnotist hasn't time to work on all the players so he singles out the jaded star striker (or, if you prefer, centre-forward). He puts his subject into a trance and tells him he has the sharpness of Gary Lineker, the strength of Maradona and the deadliness of Ian Rush (or, for those who remember, Denis Law, Geoff Hurst and Jimmy Greaves). The hypnotist snaps his fingers and tells the striker to change and go out to play the game of his life. 'Not bloody likely,' the player replies. 'I'm too good for this shower.'

Hypnotism has a powerful image. But does it work?

Towards the end of the 1948–9 season, Hinckley Athletic, sliding towards the bottom of the Birmingham Combination, set up a publicity stunt which went a little wrong, mainly because the Hinckley directors blew hot and cold about the involvement of a hypnotist. It wasn't clear whether they were in favour or not.

The advertisement in the *Hinckley Times* was clear enough about the event scheduled for the Hinckley Working Men's Club Hall on Tuesday 12 April: RICHARD PAYNE WILL CONDUCT AN AMAZING EXPERIMENT WITH MEMBERS OF THE HINCKLEY ATHLETIC TEAM. DON'T MISS IT.

Richard Payne, billed as 'Britain's Greatest Hypnotist', was apparently taking an evening off from his billing at Leicester to do a special performance in aid of an improvement scheme for Hinckley Athletic's Middlefield Lane ground.

It was also expected that Payne would contribute to an improvement scheme for events *on* the pitch. Coming up in a week's time was a game against the leaders of the Birmingham Combination, local rivals Bedworth Town.

Three hundred fans turned up at the Working Men's Club Hall to see Richard Payne put six Hinckley Athletic players to sleep. 'You will win,' he told them. 'You will win.' It was mesmerizing stuff. The left-half was so carried away that he kicked a hat a distance of 50 yards along the length of the hall.

But the scheme had a second stage. Richard Payne planned to visit the Hinckley dressing-room on Easter Tuesday, the day of the big game against Bedworth. However, the directors weren't convinced a hypnotist was needed. They were thinking in terms of a new goalkeeper or a new player-manager. Payne failed to complete his project.

Although readers of the *Hinckley Times* were implored to visit Middlefield Lane on Easter Tuesday to assess the results of 'football's most amazing experiment', Richard Payne did not actually appear in the dressing-room, and Hinckley didn't play any better. Bedworth won 2–1 and clinched the Birmingham Combination Championship in a canter. Hinckley, in fact, lost all three Easter games and continued their downward trend. At the end of the season they parted company with player-coach Bobby Davidson. There is no record of whether any hypnotists applied for the vacant post.

THE INVISIBLE GAME

SOUTHAMPTON, OCTOBER 1950

When Southampton pioneered a floodlit exhibition match against neighbours Bournemouth, about 10,000 people took advantage of the offer of free admission, but they only just got their money's worth. It was a mysterious game that no one could see properly.

The idea emerged from Southampton's summer tour of Brazil, where they played several games under artificial light. The Southampton Supporters' club, on hearing the good reports, invested £600 for a firm called B.A. Corry to install sixteen 1,500-watt arc lamps. Everyone was pleasantly surprised that electricity running costs would be as low as six or seven shillings, so the big question was whether spectators would like it. Here was the big test.

Approaching kick-off time of 6.30 pm, the crowd began to gather and exchange wisecracks.

'Bring on the shadow teams.'

'Come on Wraith Rovers.'

'Pylon the pressure.'

The spectators had to rely on their own entertainment. Although the lights worked well, visibility was destroyed by a familiar British problem – fog. That evening the whole country was enveloped in a thick mist. At London Airport a BEA Viking airliner crashed, killing all 31 people aboard.

At Southampton's ground, the Dell, the fog wasn't too much of a handicap for the players, who could see the ball

95

reasonably clearly, except when it was kicked high in the air, but the referee couldn't see a hand-ball in front of him, and the spectators were literally in the dark. At times visibility slumped to three or four yards and only nearside play could be seen.

The teams played for an hour, changing straight round without a half-time interval. For the spectators it was an eerie experience. In the damp night air, the Bournemouth players, wearing all-white, were a team of apparitions, flitting about like will-o'-the-wisps. From the stand, for all the crowd knew, the players could have been ghosts of the days when footballers wore moustaches and shin-pads outside socks – except for one two-minute period when the fog temporarily lifted and the outcome was theatrical.

There was a rumour that Southampton came close to scoring – Ken Bird pushed Eric Day's shot on to a goalpost – and the consensus was that the game finished without a goal. This was confirmed later by the players.

'Floodlit play needed infra-red glasses,' shrieked the *Daily Telegraph* headline the next day. Their reporter, Lainson Wood, was dubious about the future prospects of floodlights, saying that no one had made it pay in 20 years of dabbling, and there would always be fog.

Yet several onlookers were impressed.

'There were efforts to introduce floodlight football to this country before the war, but never anything so simple and economical as the installation at the Dell,' wrote Clifford Webb in the *Daily Herald*.

Another observer – if that is the right term for this fog-shrouded night – was Walter Winterbottom, the England team manager. 'This match,' Winterbottom was quoted as saying, 'has proved that even on a foggy night amateur players who cannot train in the daytime can get on to a pitch and have real match practice.'

Here, too, was the crux of Southampton's argument. Their chairman, Penn Barrow, pointed out that the cost of floodlights was far less than the cost of buying players. If they could produce one player from floodlight training it would have paid them.

This game, mysterious though it was to spectators, symbolized a new wave in the floodlighting movement. By the mid-1950s, lights were being used for games as well as for training.

TWO TEAMS, ONE MANAGER

YORK, OCTOBER 1952

Only a man like Dick Duckworth could manage two teams
playing in the same game. His old club, York City, were
playing his new club, Stockport County, and the game coin-
cided with his changeover.

Dick Duckworth had an exceptionally long career as a
player, manager and scout, serving more than a dozen Football League clubs. His playing career was mainly confined
to Division Three North, although he helped Chesterfield to
promotion and captained York City when they 'giant-killed'
two First Division teams and Second Division Coventry City
to reach the sixth round of the 1938 FA Cup competition. In
between, Duckworth also played for Southport, Chester and
Rotherham.

York City was Duckworth's first managerial job in the
Football League. He had been there just over two years
when he was offered a similar post at Stockport County,
Andy Beattie having moved to Huddersfield Town. The
York directors agreed to release Duckworth from his contract on 22 October 1952. His last game in charge was at
home to Stockport County. The *Yorkshire Evening Press*
described it as 'a piquant position for Mr Duckworth' and
it certainly was. That week all the players on the field would
come under his control.

Despite being third in Division Three North, York City
were having difficulty scoring goals. Supporters writing to

the local newspapers were suggesting the usual subtle tactical changes, like swopping the five forwards for those in the reserves. Dick Duckworth, a big, pipe-smoking, balding man with plenty of presence, wasn't the type to react to pressures from supporters, but, in his last week, he did bring in two reserves. Winger Bobby Warrender was introduced for his debut, and 18-year-old Dave Dunmore would play centre-forward against Stockport.

What must Dick Duckworth have thought when he saw York City overwhelm his new team? Billy Fenton scored twice and Dave Dunmore added a third, all in the first hour's play. York won 3–0, deservedly and decisively.

Duckworth learned that his new job would be a challenge. Stockport County, midway in the league table, had plenty of problems. Alf Lythgoe, who had followed Andy Beattie to Huddersfield, claimed that Stockport County were not a happy family and any new manager would have a tough job off the field. Twenty-seven Stockport players refuted this claim by signing an open letter: 'We, the undersigned players of Stockport County, resent the untrue statements under the name of Alf Lythgoe. To say that the County players are not a happy family off the field is a wicked insinuation. We are unanimous in giving the lie to this.'

In contrast to the youthful exuberance of York players like Dunmore, who was soon to attract a £10,000 cheque from Tottenham Hotspur, the Stockport County first team had an average age of 30.

Dick Duckworth never achieved promotion for Stockport County in his four years with the club, and his next club, Darlington, were similarly established in Division Three North. However, in his fourth Football League management job, Duckworth came close to achieving something no one had done and probably ever will do. Any manager who can come within five Second Division points of taking Scunthorpe United into the First Division, as Duckworth did in 1961–2, deserves to manage both teams in more than one game.

RECORD SCORE

MANCHESTER, AUTUMN 1952

To score more than 20 goals in a game is a phenomenal achievement, one that usually requires a special set of circumstances. The standards for high scoring were set in the last century – Aberdeen's 36–0 Scottish Cup win against Bon Accord and Preston North End's 26–0 win against Hyde in the FA Cup – but there have been some good attempts in recent years.

In the inaugural year of the FA Youth Cup (1952–3), Manchester United were drawn away to Nantwich Town. In his book *Centenary Dabbers*, a history of Nantwich Town, Michael Chatwin tells how Nantwich accepted Matt Busby's offer of £50 to switch the game to the Cliff at Broughton, where the match was played under floodlights. Manchester United loaned Nantwich a set of yellow fluorescent shirts but the Cheshire lads were rarely seen. United were able to call on their Busby Babes, youths like Eddie Colman, Duncan Edwards, David Pegg and Billy Whelan, all of whom lost their lives in the tragic Munich Disaster. They beat Nantwich 23–0 and Edwards scored five from wing-half. But, of course, it was a case of the Nantwich goalkeeper keeping the score down. United were so impressed with George Westwell that they signed him after the game.

Manchester United totally dominated the FA Youth Cup in its early years, winning the trophy five seasons in succession, and this was simply a case of one team being 23 goals

better than the other. Some exceptionally high scores, however, are achieved in more suspicious circumstances. *The
Guinness Book of Records* quotes a couple of examples
from Yugoslavian football in 1979. Two teams competing
with each other for promotion colluded with their respective
opponents to improve their goal differences. One won 134–1,
the other a mere 88–0.

In the early 1950s an Argentinian team called Wanderers
staged a 'sit-down strike' on their pitch, allowing their opponents to win 71–0.

Perhaps the best example of high-scoring was that achieved
by two Baden village teams at Frankfurt, West Germany, in
1949. Promised a bottle of schnapps for every goal scored,
the teams put on a dazzling exhibition of attacking play. The
result – 25 to 24.

THE 44-MINUTE GAME

COVENTRY, JANUARY 1956

If a player is sent off by the referee but refuses to leave the field then the referee should abandon the match. Arthur Ellis, an international referee from Halifax, did exactly that after 44 minutes of a floodlight friendly between Coventry City and San Lorenzo, an Argentinian club on tour in Britain.

Referring to tempestuous games as 'friendlies' is always a cheap joke, so perhaps the comparative American term 'exhibition game' is better suited. It was a real exhibition.

It started well enough and, as half-time approached, with the score 1–1, most people felt it had the potential to be a great game. Then Arthur Ellis, a Cup Final referee in 1952, awarded Coventry a penalty for a push on Dennis Uphill. Ellis was surrounded by Argentinians and kicked by teenage inside-left Jose Sanfilippo, who was sent off.

Sanfilippo refused to leave the field. Two team-mates tried to pull him off, three tried to keep him on. Interpreters, police and San Lorenzo officials were soon on the pitch. Arthur Ellis abandoned the match and stuck by his decision.

Coventry City chairman Erle Shanks had the task of announcing the news to the 17,000 crowd: 'Mr Ellis, the referee, states that he was kicked by the San Lorenzo player Sanfilippo. He immediately ordered the player to the dressing-room. The player refused to go and was supported in his attitude by certain of their players. Under the

102

circumstances Mr Ellis has abandoned the game as he refuses to referee under these impossible conditions. Under FA rules we are not allowed to appoint a substitute.'

This was the fifth game of San Lorenzo's tour. They were finding it hard to adjust to the British mud and had yet to win. They had played Brentford, Rangers, Sheffield Wednesday, Wolves and now Coventry. Their sixth and last game was on a frozen pitch at Southampton, where San Lorenzo won 2–1. By that time San Lorenzo officials and Sanfilippo had apologized to Coventry City.

Jose Sanfilippo, whose stubbornness was described by Ellis as akin to that of a mule, had an interesting career. He was always scoring goals and always temperamental. He played for Argentina in the 1958 World Cup and was the country's top League goalscorer for four successive seasons (1958 to 1961). Finally, San Lorenzo, finding him difficult to handle, transferred him to Boca Juniors for £85,000, the sort of money AC Milan were paying for Jimmy Greaves. Sanfilippo had success there, until he attacked the team coach. He moved on, continuing his chequered career until he returned to San Lorenzo in his late thirties. He had settled down by then.

SECOND-HALF TRANSFORMATION

LONDON, DECEMBER 1957

It was the Saturday before Christmas. Many of Charlton Athletic's regular supporters had opted for Christmas shopping rather than the home game against Huddersfield Town. Still more did the same after an hour's play. Charlton were losing 5–1 and were down to ten players. It didn't seem worth staying until the end. But let that be a warning. Those who left early missed a most amazing transformation.

In those days Charlton Athletic played at the Valley, a huge stadium capable of holding 70,000, and on this pre-Christmas Saturday it looked fairly empty with only 12,500 spectators inside. At half-time Charlton were 2–0 down and not playing well. They had also lost centre-half Derek Ufton, who had dislocated a shoulder, and would have to play with ten men for the last 80 minutes of the game. No substitutes were allowed at that time.

The one man who will be forever associated with Charlton Athletic's stunning transformation that day was Johnny Summers, their tall, stocky outside-left. At half-time he changed his boots, thinking it would be a good time to break in a new pair. After all, Charlton had little chance, and his old pair of boots were falling to pieces.

In the third minute of the second half Summers scored his first goal, but Huddersfield Town popped in three more and led 5–1 after an hour. The visitors, who included future England full-back Ray Wilson and England international wing-half Bill McGarry, looked certainties for two Second Division points, even when John 'Buck' Ryan scored a consolation goal.

Then Johnny Summers scored four goals. In the rearrangements following Ufton's injury, Summers had moved to centre-forward. It was from this position that he scored his goals, all with his unnatural right foot, all wearing his new boots. The remaining spectators were rewarded for their loyalty. They were going berserk and there were still ten minutes to play, Charlton leading 6–5. Then Huddersfield equalized.

The winning goal came with the last shot of the match. Charlton's Fred Lucas fed John Ryan and the big attacker slammed the 11th goal of the second half. Charlton had won 7–6. Moments later, when the final whistle went, the crowd began calling for the players and Johnny Summers in particular. 'We want Summers,' they chanted. At length the players appeared in the directors' box, and were greeted rapturously.

Meanwhile, in the Miller Hospital at Greenwich, the injured Derek Ufton could hardly believe what he was hearing. 7–6? It couldn't have been the game he started off in. It wasn't until team-mate Stuart Leary visited him at the hospital that Ufton could take in the news.

There was a strange sequel less than three weeks later. Charlton Athletic and Huddersfield Town met in an FA Cup third-round replay at the same place, the Valley. A much bigger crowd turned out, expecting a repeat of the goal glut. Charlton won 1–0.

THE TRIPLICATED CUP-TIE

LEEDS, JANUARY 1958

In 1955–6, in the third round of the FA Cup, Leeds United were drawn at home to Cardiff City.

In 1956–7, in the third round of the FA Cup, Leeds United were drawn at home to Cardiff City.

In 1957–8, in the third round of the FA Cup, Leeds United were drawn at home to Cardiff City.

Had the possibility been suggested before the 1955–6 third-round draw that Leeds would be at home to Cardiff in three successive seasons, a statistician would have calculated the odds at one in two million. Yet something even more unlikely occurred. Let's look at the results.

In 1955–6, Cardiff City won 2–1 at Leeds after a goalless first half.

In 1956–7, Cardiff City won 2–1 at Leeds after a goalless first half.

In January 1958, therefore, there was a sense of *déjà vu* when 30,374 people visited Elland Road, Leeds, to see the third third-round meeting in successive seasons. Surely Leeds must now gain revenge. The status of the clubs had been reversed. Whereas Cardiff were in the First Division and Leeds in the Second in January 1956, the roles were now the opposite, Leeds promoted, Cardiff relegated. When the teams had met in the First Division, in 1956–7, Leeds had cruised to a 3–0 home victory. It was virtually impossible for three successive 2–1 away wins to occur.

Or was it?

The conditions were icy and precarious. Second Division Cardiff scored first, Alan Harrington scoring from long range in the 20th minute. Bobby Forrest equalized with a header from Wilbur Cush's centre and Leeds took control. Right on half-time, however, came a second Cardiff goal, Cliff Nugent being the scorer. At half-time Cardiff led by the magic, magnetic 2–1 scoreline.

Surely it couldn't happen again – but it did. The referee had the best chance to prevent a 2–1 Cardiff win, when, in the last minute, Wilbur Cush was brought down and Leeds appealed for a penalty. It was not given. Cardiff won 2–1 – three times in a row.

This was the sixth of ten successive seasons which saw Leeds United knocked out of the FA Cup at the third round. But I wouldn't want to leave the impression that Cardiff City are Leeds United's jinx team. On the other four occasions they have been drawn together in the FA Cup, Leeds were the winners on every occasion, and they have lost only one of 15 home League games. All of which makes Cardiff's hat trick of away third-round victories one of soccer's strangest events.

SIX IN A ROW TO STAY UP

LINCOLN, MAY 1958

Shortly after the 3–1 home defeat by Barnsley on Easter Monday, when Lincoln City were all but mathematically certain of relegation with six games to play, Lincoln manager Bill Anderson explained to his players how they stood: 'If we win our last six games we'll stay up.'

Ho, ho, very funny. Lincoln had not won for four months and had won only five of their 36 Second Division matches that season. This could only be the talk of a desperate manager. Anderson, who had been in charge of Lincoln for twelve seasons, the last six in the Second Division, was in his toughest spot yet.

The fixture-list left Lincoln with three away games and three at home. There were no outstanding teams among the opponents – two or three were also needing points for safety – but all the fixtures were psychologically daunting, including the first of the six, away to Barnsley on Easter Tuesday, the day after suffering that resounding defeat at home to the same team.

The strangest fixture, though, was the last of the season – Cardiff City at home. That one had already been lost. Back in March Cardiff had been winning 3–0 at Lincoln when a blizzard wiped out the play and caused an abandonment. The teams would have to start again, but Cardiff had already won the game once.

Bill Anderson made four changes for the return game at

Barnsley, and his new-look team won 3–1. Then Lincoln won 3–1 at second-from-bottom Doncaster and beat Rotherham (2–0) and Bristol City (4–0) at home. They were left needing a win and a draw from their last two games.

The away game at Huddersfield was their most difficult game on paper, but Ron Harbertson's sixth goal in five games brought a 1–0 victory. All that remained was the home game with Cardiff City. Had the game been completed in March, when Cardiff led 3–0, manager Anderson's Easter pep talk wouldn't have made as much sense. Lincoln would have needed to win six of their last five games to escape relegation.

The whole city had caught the spirit of Lincoln's five-match run. It was as though it was a Cup run which had taken them to the final. Inside-forward George Hannah described the tension before the Cardiff game, when over 18,000 people packed into the tiny Sincil Bank stadium, as worse than when he played at Wembley with Newcastle United.

Just after half-time Cliff Nugent scored for Cardiff. Lincoln, playing edgily, looked doomed to Division Three. For the second time that season Cardiff appeared to have an away game at Lincoln firmly in control.

There were 20 minutes to play when Roy Chapman lunged for a centre and levelled the scores. Chapman, who had regained his place in the team at start of this run, scored again soon afterwards. Harbertson scored a third from 20 yards, and the crowd roared as if Lincoln City had won the FA Cup. Three goals in 10 minutes.

Lincoln, 3–0 down to Cardiff when the game was abandoned in March, 1–0 down after 70 minutes of the replay, beat Cardiff 3–1 and avoided relegation by a point. They had won their last six games, and Bill Anderson had got it exactly right.

GIANT-KILLING GLORY

WORCESTER, JANUARY 1959

A director of a Fourth Division club once arrived at the stadium on the afternoon of a home tie against attractive First Division opposition. He surveyed the 'icebergs' and ruts at one end of the pitch and the mud and straw at the other and gave his opinion about the obvious postponement. 'Get the referee to play it,' he told the secretary. 'We can beat them on this.'

Ah, the beauty of the British weather in January, the glory of the FA Cup. No book on strange matches would be complete without at least one giant-killing act, where a small club produces an odd result against a big club.

Not all giant-killing, however, is strange. Some teams, like Peterborough United and Swindon Town in the 1960s, were so good at it that people turned up expecting an upset. Some had such good giant-killing years that they almost went the distance. One thinks of Millwall (1937), Port Vale (1954), York City (1955), Norwich City (1959) and Crystal Palace (1976), all of whom reached the semi-final. Certain top clubs create a reputation for being vulnerable. Newcastle United may have won three post-war FA Cup Finals but they have also lost home draws to a galaxy of lower-division teams – Bradford Park Avenue, Rotherham, Scunthorpe, Peterborough, Bedford Town, Carlisle United, Hereford United (in a replay), Wrexham (in a replay), Chester and Exeter City (in a replay). In a year when they did get to Wembley (1974),

110

Newcastle started their Cup run by drawing 1–1 at home to Hendon. The result was almost predictable.

One of the glamorous features about the FA Cup is that it can create fixtures which are strange (whatever the result): Tooting & Mitcham against Nottingham Forest (1959), Ashington against Aston Villa (1924), Manchester United against Walthamstow Avenue (1953), Lovell's Athletic against Wolverhampton Wanderers (1946), and so on. When a non-League team beats First Division opposition it is front-page news – for instance, Colchester United against Huddersfield (1948), Yeovil against Sunderland (1949), Hereford against Newcastle (1972) and Sutton United against Coventry City (1989).

I have chosen a third-round FA Cup tie on the edge of that pack, one perhaps less remembered, but which, in my opinion, captures the essence of the FA Cup and the vagaries of the British weather. Southern League Worcester City were hosts to Second Division promotion favourites Liverpool, who had lost only two of their last 16 games. Ground conditions for the Saturday of the game were typical Cup-tie conditions. Worcester cleared the snow from the pitch, which then froze. The referee postponed the game.

They tried again the following Thursday. Liverpool had to return tickets they couldn't sell and Worcester City sold them. The crowd was more partisan, the pitch still frozen, the ball erratic in its bounce and not easy to control. In the 10th minute Liverpool full-back John Molyneux tried a back-pass, goalkeeper Tommy Younger did his best to reach it, Worcester's 18-year-old Tommy Skuse skated after it, put the ball in the net and promptly fell over.

Worcester's second goal, in the 82nd minute, was just as unfortunate for the Liverpool defence. Harry Knowles crossed hard from the right, Liverpool centre-half Dick White kicked at the centre and the ball flew over goalkeeper Younger for an own-goal. A minute later Liverpool pulled back a goal, Geoff Twentyman scoring from a penalty.

The last few minutes seemed like hours to Worcester fans. When the final whistle went, the score still 2–1, they swarmed on to the field to congratulate their heroes, throwing hats in the air, engulfing the blue-and-white-shirted players, lifting up goalkeeper Johnny Kirkwood and captain Roy Paul and carrying them from the field. Paul had captained Manchester City when they won the 1956 FA Cup Final.

Worcester City manager Bill Thompson, who had made a few appearances for Portsmouth in the Championship-winning seasons of 1948-9 and 1949-50, could feel proud of his team's gritty performance. The pitch aside, Worcester had played determinedly and won deservedly. That season Worcester set three record attendances for the St George's Lane ground, the first against Millwall in the second round, the last when Sheffield United won 2-0 in the fourth round. Their Cup run should be remembered for the day Worcester City inflicted one of the strangest defeats in Liverpool's history.

THE MISSING FUSES

WATFORD, APRIL 1959

There are several games in which floodlight failure has led to long delays or even abandonments, but perhaps one of the most mysterious was the Watford-Shrewsbury clash close to the end of the 1958–9 season.

Shrewsbury Town were challenging for promotion, occupying fourth place in the new Fourth Division, but they had little to spare and were closely scrutinizing the goal average of fifth-placed Exeter City. Two days after this Watford game, Shrewsbury would face Exeter at home.

Watford, a mid-table team, had little to play for except the end of the season. At half-time they were losing 4–1 to Shrewsbury, having conceded two own-goals on a pitch which was hard, bumpy and of unpredictable bounce.

Halfway through the second half the floodlight suddenly went off. It transpired later that three fuses had been removed. Not a case of sabotage, the police believed, more a case of larceny.

It was an evening game. There was still some natural light, but not enough. Nevertheless, referee Denis Howell started the game again. Meanwhile, club officials tried to do what they could with the floodlights, a bit daunting given the notice on the doors: DANGER, HIGH VOLTAGE ELECTRICITY. Fuse thieves must know what they are doing.

The pitch was virtually in darkness, but the teams did

113

their best to play on. Spectators tried to help by lighting newspapers. Watford's Peter Walker shot from 35 yards and nobody thought to warn Shrewsbury goalkeeper Russell Crossley that a ball was on its way. It flew past him into the net. Then Colin Whitaker scored one at the other end. Shrewsbury led 5–2, but conditions were impossible. Recognizing the risk of injury, referee Howell abandoned the game after 76 minutes.

Shrewsbury claimed it was floodlight robbery as they needed those two points and five goals for their promotion prospects. The Watford club was fined £100 by the Football League for failing to ensure their floodlights were in order. The game had to be played again. The Football League said it should be played in daylight hours.

When Shrewsbury returned to Watford in the first week in May, having meantime beaten Exeter City by three goals from player-manager Arthur Rowley, they needed a point to guarantee promotion. There was a sense of justice about the result. Shrewsbury beat Watford 4–1, exactly the score when the floodlights failed in the previous abandoned game. They were promoted to Division Three, where they stayed for the next 15 seasons.

'FANTASTIC, INCREDIBLE, AMAZING'

LONDON, OCTOBER 1960

Cliff Mitchell, sports reporter on the Middlesbrough *Evening Gazette*, ran out of superlatives when describing the Division Two game between Charlton Athletic and Middlesbrough: 'fantastic, incredible, amazing . . . it was rumbustious, dynamic fare and it stirred the blood . . . I can't imagine a more thrilling tussle than this one. It will live for years.'

All the ingredients were right. It was early enough in the season for teams to be carefree, energetic and optimistic. The relentless rain produced a slippery grassy surface which encouraged a fast pace. Both teams were in goalscoring form – Charlton had won 5–3 at Brighton the previous week, Middlesbrough had recently chalked up high-scoring draws at Leeds (4–4) and Plymouth (3–3) – and both clubs had a goalscoring tradition. Charlton had averaged almost 100 goals a season since they slipped into Division Two in 1957, Middlesbrough had scored over 80 goals in each of their last four seasons.

There were also some special goalscorers in action. Brian Clough, Middlesbrough's England-international centre-forward, maintained a phenomenal strike rate. The player alongside him, Alan Peacock, would also play for England and command a high transfer fee from Leeds United. Charlton had two men, Stuart Leary and Johnny Summers,

115

who would end their careers with over 150 Football League goals.

There were enough incidents in the first 13 minutes to satisfy many crowds for a whole game. Yet there were no goals from this hectic start. Once the teams started scoring the game went out of control. Eleven goals in 54 minutes: Eddie Werge (1–0 to Charlton after 13), Brian Clough (1–1 after 15), Ron Burbeck (2–1 to Middlesbrough after 17), Dennis Edwards (2–2 after 21), Stuart Leary (3–2 to Charlton after 28), Derek McLean (3–3 after 29), Clough again (4–3 to Middlesbrough after 30), Edwards again (4–4 at half-time), Burbeck (5–4 to Middlesbrough after 49), Clough for his hat-trick (6–4 after 63), Edwards for his hat-trick (6–5 to Middlesbrough after 69 minutes).

The finale was saved for the last minute. Johnny Summers dropped a centre in the Middlesbrough goalmouth. A swarm of muddy players challenged hungrily. Somehow the ball ended in the net without touching anyone. A real old-fashioned goal to end a real old-fashioned game. Six goals each. Fantastic, incredible, amazing.

THE DISALLOWED DOUBLE HAT-TRICK

LUTON, JANUARY 1961

On a day of relentless rain, on a pitch of mainly mud, Denis Law scored six successive goals in 50 minutes to help Manchester City into a 6–2 lead against Luton Town. Unfortunately for Law and Manchester City, the referee abandoned the game after 69 minutes. Luton and Manchester City had to start their fourth-round FA Cup tie again the following Wednesday.

The first meeting had plenty of strange twists. Luton started so well that they were 2–0 ahead after 17 minutes, Alec Ashworth scoring both. Then came Law's spectacular show. The Scottish international showed incredible close-range reactions as he headed and flicked in anything that was in the goal-area, taking advantage of defenders floundering in the mud. One hat-trick was followed by another, but, all the time, there were doubts about whether the pitch was fit. Finally, after 69 minutes, referee Ken Tuck of Chesterfield abandoned the game.

The second attempt started similarly to the first, Luton scoring twice in the first 22 minutes. Denis Law scored for Manchester City just before half-time, but this time there were no hat-tricks to follow. Ashworth's second-half goal sealed a 3–1 victory for Luton, although, overall, Manchester

City had scored seven (Law seven) and Luton only five (Ashworth four and Fleming one).

Luton lost 1–0 at Third Division Barnsley in the fifth round.

THE NIGHTMARE DAY-TRIP

BARROW, OCTOBER 1961

Gillingham thought they could travel to Barrow on the day of the game. The journey from the mouth of Kent's River Medway to the tip of the Furness peninsula in Lancashire (as it was then) was over 300 miles. A train leaving London Euston at 9.05 am seemed a safe bet. The team should arrive over an hour before kick-off, which was at 5.15 pm as Barrow had no floodlights.

First came the 35-mile coach trip to Euston. The coach made an early-morning start but ran into heavy traffic. Officials estimated the time-distance equation and grew agitated. The coach arrived at Euston half an hour after the train had left.

The options remaining were not promising. The next train, the 10.25, would arrive one minute after the kick-off. Coach would be far too slow, and cars would be very risky. There was only one possible option – aeroplane. Club officials discovered two suitable scheduled flights – the 10.40 to Manchester and the 11.00 to Newcastle. Both were fully booked.

The next idea was to charter a plane. One was arranged but the company had to fly it from Gatwick to London Airport, where the Gillingham party would be waiting. The cost of the plane was £500 – money in advance.

Gillingham officials also telephoned the Football League. They negotiated a 15-minute delay in kick-off time. The players would be asked to forego their half-time interval. It was a 5.30 pm kick-off now.

The next problem was the plane's destination. They decided to head for Squire's Gate Airport at Blackpool, about 70 miles from Barrow. This meant arranging another journey. A coach was hired to meet them at Squire's Gate, but, as time slipped by, officials realized a coach would be too slow. Four cars were hired and a police escort arranged for what would be a hectic last leg of the trip.

The charter flight left London Airport at 2.31, having been delayed in a queue of planes. There were less than three hours before the match.

The plane arrived at Squire's Gate at 3.25 pm. Within 20 minutes everybody was in cars. They had a 70-mile journey and 105 minutes.

There were no motorways in the north-west in October 1961. The roads around Morecambe Bay were among the country's worst for a late dash by car through driving rain. They reached Holker Street at 5.30 pm. The players needed to change.

Gillingham, as you can appreciate, were not ideally prepared to play a Fourth Division game. They'd been up early, stuck in traffic on a coach, forced to hang around, shepherded on to a plane (the first time for some), driven rapidly through the countryside and told to change as quickly as they could. By half-time they were five goals down to Barrow.

The problem now was the light. By the 74th minute, when Barrow were leading 6–0, referee Mr Jobling from Morecambe felt it was too dark for football. He allowed an extra couple of minutes under Barrow's training lights – just time for Barrow's seventh goal – but finally abandoned the game shortly after seven o'clock.

The Football League ruled that the 7–0 scoreline should stand as a result. Gillingham's next away game was an even longer trip – Carlisle United. They set off in good time and won 2–1.

FAREWELL IN A BLIZZARD

CREWE, MARCH 1962

Crewe in the snow. It seemed like the last place on earth, and it was, literally, for the visitors. A few days later Accrington Stanley died. This was the club's final fixture.

As a game, it was ordinarily one-sided. Crewe's Terry Tighe, a former Accrington player, sportingly did his best to give his former club a first-minute boost – his back-pass was cleared off the goal-line – but thereafter it was one-way traffic towards the Accrington goal. Probably the coldest man in Crewe that day was Jack Ferguson, the home-team goalkeeper, who was stranded alone in a snowstorm as Crewe scored four times at the other end.

Accrington Stanley were saved from an even bigger defeat than 4–0 by goalkeeper Alex Smith, who, according to one report, was in 'the £15,000 class' (not far below the £23,500 Harry Gregg goalkeeping record) and whose penalty save at Doncaster in the previous game had earned Accrington Stanley their last-ever Fourth Division point. Smith nearly didn't play at Crewe, relying on a late dash by car to join the team at Knutsford after missing the team coach. He had just moved into a new house and must have been looking forward to a career with his new club. A few days later he was out of a job.

On the Monday after the Friday game at Crewe, Accrington Stanley held a meeting of creditors. The news was worse than anyone had anticipated. Unsecured creditors were owed over £43,000 (more than the cost of Brian Clough's big news transfer from Middlesbrough to Sunderland around the same time) and the club had total debts of around £60,000. Accrington Stanley could no longer compete with the seven Lancashire clubs in the First Division. Stanley resigned from the Football League. The league had lost one of its founder members.

The directors had been paying players' wages for many months. Now they needed an immediate £400 to prevent the cutting-off of telephone, gas, electricity and water. When the players reported on Tuesday they were told the sad news, but no training was possible anyway – the water pipes were frozen. The players stood around and kicked their heels while a tradesman's van came to collect the club's washing-machine.

After three days of mourning there was another attempt to resurrect the club with yet another 'Save Stanley' campaign. There was no success. The Football League refused to rescind Accrington Stanley's resignation. The club had played its last game on a snowy, eerie night in Crewe.

A SPORTS SCANDAL

IPSWICH, DECEMBER 1962

It was an ordinary First Division game, not particularly memorable. Two goals by Ray Crawford gave Ipswich Town a 2–0 victory over Sheffield Wednesday. The win helped Ipswich move out of the bottom two. Wednesday, in the top half of the table, should have had something more tangible to show from the 15 corner-kicks they won during the game.

It was 16 months before the game came to national prominence. A team of *Sunday People* investigators, led by Michael Gabbert, revealed what they called 'the biggest sports scandal of the century'. The newspaper alleged that three Sheffield Wednesday players had put bets on their own team to lose.

Criminal investigations were started. In January 1965, ten players (or ex-players) were sent to prison for conspiracy to defraud in fixing matches. Jimmy Gauld, called 'the ringleader' by the *Sunday People*, was sentenced to four years' imprisonment with £5,000 costs. 'You have befouled professional football and corrupted your friends and acquaintances,' he was told by Justice Lawton at Nottingham. Evidence showed that Gauld, who had played for Waterford, Charlton, Everton, Plymouth, Swindon, St Johnstone and Mansfield, had made £3,275 from betting on matches and £7,420 from the *Sunday People* for his story.

Three Sheffield Wednesday players, David 'Bronco' Layne, Tony Kay and Peter Swan, all received four-month

123

sentences. This virtually ended their careers, although Swan had his life ban lifted and returned to play for Sheffield Wednesday in 1972–3. Simon Inglis, in his book *Soccer in the Dock*, gives a more detailed account of this soccer scandal and many others. What is strange is that, according to newspaper reports, Tony Kay, then being watched by a number of clubs, was Sheffield Wednesday's star against Ipswich. Later the same month (December 1962) Kay joined Everton for £55,000, and he ended the season with a League Championship medal.

ALL IN THE IMAGINATION

FORFAR, FEBRUARY 1963

'It was a great game at Station Park on Saturday although few spectators braved the elements. Three seagulls and a dead sparrow occupied the enclosure, while the only spectator in the stand besides the "Dispatch" reporter was a dispossessed field-mouse.'

That was how the *Forfar Dispatch* introduced its report of the imaginary game between Forfar Athletic and Stirling Albion during the big-freeze winter of 1962–3. Snow and ice layered the pitches and terraces, matches were postponed *en masse* and a major casualty was the football pools, until the introduction of a pools panel to fix the results of imaginary games.

The pools companies first disclosed the plan in the third week of January. If there were more than 30 postponements a panel of experts would forecast results of games postponed – home win, away win or draw. (In the 1960s, 0–0 draws counted the same as other draws in pools points.) Doubts about the legality of the scheme were overcome and a panel brought into action. It consisted of Lord Brabazon of Tara (chair) and four ex-international players, Ted Drake, Tom Finney, Tommy Lawton and George Young.

The objectives of the scheme were very clear – to help the pools companies and provide a continuing outlet for the nation's gambling impulses. This was little consolation for non-gambling soccer fans, who had no chance of following a game . . . unless they read the *Forfar Dispatch*. The reporter took the panel's imaginary result and unearthed an imaginary game which was exciting from the very start.

'Straight from the first blast of the imaginary referee's kid-on whistle, Albion swept into the attack. Lawlor, scrambling over a large heap of salt in the Forfar goal-area, got his boot to a loose ball but kicked it high over the bar. Play was held up for five minutes while the luckless inside-right, assisted by his team-mates, searched for his boot in the adjacent field.'

You get the idea?

You are given the result – in this case an away win to Stirling Albion – and you write the match report to fit the result. I'm surprised more reporters don't try it.

The *Forfar Dispatch* spared us no details. We learn about the first goal – scored by Park while the Forfar goalkeeper had his foot caught in the side-netting – and the three incidents needing the non-existent trainer's magic sponge: Dick shot over the bar and landed heavily when he came down on the other side; Cumming, in agony, pink in the face, clutching his stomach, needed a new piece of elastic for his shorts; and a Forfar forward, through on his own, hit the post, and was carried off with a nasty bump on his forehead.

Reid scored Forfar's equalizer – his colleagues pelted the Stirling goalkeeper with snowballs – and it was 1–1 at the end of the first half, which lasted for 63 minutes as the referee had difficulty defrosting the pea in his whistle.

Both teams scored early in the second half. Soon Forfar led by the odd goal in five, and a very odd goal it was, scored by Dick, who tied his boot-lace to the football-lace and ran 50 yards into the net. An excellent imaginary pass by Stirling's Fish started Stirling's recovery. They went 4–3 ahead but Forfar equalized. Four-four. Time running out. The *Forfar Dispatch* captured those last tense moments with typical brilliance: 'Forfar officials were already on the phone to London to tell the panel of pools experts that the game was an imaginary draw when, in the dying minutes, Johnstone notched up number five for the visitors, a kid-on away win.'

The reporter added a footnote about the Stirling Albion defender who, on hearing his team had been awarded an away win, went to his manager and asked for his win bonus. 'Surely, I must have told you,' said the quick-thinking manager. 'You were dropped for that game.'

All fiction, perhaps, but this imaginary game had its roots in the reality of a pools-panel away win. From the town that had once provided one of football's most alliterative 5–4 results – Forfar five East Fife four (try saying that in a hurry) – now came the most vivid account of an imaginary 5–4 result. And, just for the record, the pools panel had it correct. When the teams met later in the season Stirling Albion recorded an away win. The score, though, was 2–0.

THE ABANDONED INTERNATIONAL

GLASGOW, MAY 1963

The Scotland-Austria international match at Hampden Park, watched by over 94,000 people, began to simmer in the 16th minute when Davie Wilson scored for Scotland. Austrian players had noticed the linesman's raised flag. Referee Jim Finney waved aside their protests.

After Wilson's second goal, ten minutes later, Austrian centre-forward Nemec was sent off for protesting too much. That left ten Austrians against eleven Scots, and the Scots led 2–0 in goals. By half-time Denis Law added a third goal.

Early in the second half Austria lost the injured Rafreider, who was taken from the field on a stretcher. The teams had agreed to substitute outfield players until half-time and goal-keepers at any time. Rafreider was an outfield player. That left nine Austrians against eleven Scots, and the Scots led 3–0 in goals.

Denis Law scored a fourth Scotland goal, his second of the game. Linhart scored one for Austria. Then came another unsavoury incident. Hof was sent off for a violent tackle. That left eight Austrians against eleven Scots, and the Scots led 4–1 in goals.

After more eruptions referee Finney decided he had had enough. He abandoned the game after 79 minutes, not wanting anyone else to be hurt. After all, it was a 'friendly'.

THE GAME IN TWO GROUNDS

CARDIFF AND COVENTRY, OCTOBER 1965

The Football League Division Two game between Cardiff City and Coventry City, watched by 12,639 people in Cardiff and 10,295 people in Coventry, was the first of its kind in Britain. It was relayed by closed-circuit television.

Immediately after Coventry's reserve game on Tuesday evening, the day before the game at Cardiff, workmen went into action at Highfield Road to erect scaffolding and four large screens, each 40 ft by 30 ft. Three screens faced the Sky Blue Stand, Coventry's main stand. Work went on through the night and was completed with little time to spare, minutes before the 7.30 pm kick-off at Cardiff.

The technical details, arranged by Intertel and Viewsport, were a success. The commentary was conducted by John Camkin, a journalist and Coventry City director, and Danny Blanchflower, former Spurs captain and a *Sunday Express* columnist. Coventry City obligingly switched to a set of red-and-white striped shirts, borrowed from Stoke City, to provide a more distinct contrast with Cardiff shirts.

The crowd at Highfield Road cheered as loudly as that at Ninian Park, especially when George Curtis gave Coventry the lead shortly before half-time.

During the second half, fog hung around Highfield Road, but the spectators of the screen were rarely distracted. Cardiff equalized through Gareth Williams in the 55th minute and Coventry's hopes of a first away win of the season

129

lessened. Then, three minutes from the end, Coventry scored the winner, a low shot from Welshman Ronnie Rees.

It was an exciting time in Coventry. Students were arriving at the new University of Warwick, and Coventry City were pushing towards Division One under the idea-laden leadership of manager Jimmy Hill and chairman Derrick Robins. Everything was Sky Blue – the Sky Blue Stand, the Sky Blue Train, the Sky Blue Shop, Radio Sky Blue, Sky Blue Caterers, the Sky Blue Song and, of course, Sky Blue Shirts.

Sky Blue closed-circuit television was the latest success, but the games would require very careful selection, needing to be between clubs some distance apart, so that away fans would not be prevented from travelling, and in order not to clash with other matches nearby. That would leave two or three midweek games a season at the most.

A PAIR OF BROKEN LEGS

CHESTER, JANUARY 1966

One of soccer's strangest coincidences occurred on New Year's Day 1966 when Chester full-backs Ray Jones and Bryn Jones both broke their left legs in the home game with Aldershot.

There were four players called Jones on the pitch that fateful day – Les was a Chester forward and David was the Aldershot goalkeeper – and, by the 55th minute, when the second injury happened, the others must have been wondering about their destinies.

The first accident occurred in the 21st minute. Bryn Jones tackled Derek Norman as the Aldershot forward carried the ball away. Jones was lying injured when Aldershot's Tony Priscott headed the game's opening goal. But the goal was followed by a bizarre incident – two Aldershot players seemingly fighting each other. Aldershot manager Dave Smith later explained that Norman thought he was being attacked by a Chester player rather than congratulated by a team-mate. Bryn Jones was treated for his leg fracture and taken to hospital.

Chester, with David Read on as substitute, took the initiative and showed why they were chasing promotion from the Fourth Division. Hugh Ryden scored two goals, including a 30-yard shot, and Chester had a 2–1 half-time lead.

Aldershot's Ken Maloy equalized five minutes after half-time. Then came the second tragedy of the day. Ray Jones broke his leg making a tackle, and the next time the two Chester full-backs lined up together was in a hospital ward. On the pitch, Chester, now with ten men, contrived a memorable winning goal for Mick Metcalf.

Despite this 3–2 success, Chester's promotion challenge began to fall away. They were handicapped by the loss of their two regular full-backs for the rest of the season, and were left to digest the peculiarities of the Aldershot game when both full-backs, both called Jones, both broke their left legs.

THE POPULAR NORTH KOREANS

LIVERPOOL, JUNE 1966

Some people thought it ridiculous that a team of no-hopers like North Korea could be allowed to qualify for the 1966 World Cup Finals, whereas other, more proven nations, like Czechoslovakia, Yugoslavia and Scotland, would not be there. Nobody who followed the World Cup Finals in England stuck to that opinion.

North Korea predictably lost to Russia in their first game, but gained a 1–1 draw with Chile from a late equalizer. That was nothing compared with the final match in their group. A goal from Pak Du-ik beat Italy, the group favourites. The Italians, surprisingly eliminated, did their best to sneak back home at one o'clock in the morning, at an unscheduled airfield, but their players were still hit by a torrent of tomatoes.

North Korea's progress to the quarter-final set up an astonishing match with Portugal, one of the most sporting and delightfully entertaining teams of the tournament. Portugal were also one of the favourites for the trophy, bristling with talented players like Simoes, Eusebio and Torres, the latter's height expected to provide problems for the North Koreans, none of whom were over 5 ft 8 in tall.

After 24 minutes the North Koreans led 3–0, a dazzling display of bustling, intricate short-passing football with powerful finishing. The Goodison Park crowd took them to their hearts just as those at Middlesbrough had during the group matches.

133

The game was transformed by Eusebio. Born and raised in Mozambique, a Portuguese colony until 1975, Eusebio had developed into one of the world's stars and was at his peak in this World Cup, if not this game. Dubbed the European Pele, or the Black Panther, by British newspapers, he had a superb physique, electrifying pace, a deft dribbling touch and a vicious shot. He showed it all this day.

Before half-time Eusebio scored twice, one virtually on his own, the other a penalty. Urgently, he picked the ball out of the net, ran with it back to the centre spot and handed it over, aware that Portugal had time and goals to make up. Eusebio equalized on the hour and scored his fourth from a penalty, taken with typical power. He made the fifth for Augusta. Portugal won 5–3.

The idea of two foreign international teams playing at Goodison Park was strange, that one of them should be North Korea was downright peculiar, but the outcome was memorable.

THE FANTASTIC CHAMPIONSHIP DECIDER

LOS ANGELES, JULY 1967

When Wolverhampton Wanderers (alias Los Angeles Wolves) met Aberdeen (alias Washington Whips) in a decider for the United Soccer Association Championship, the game lasted 126 minutes. There were 11 goals, including four in one three-minute spell, a sending-off and three penalties. Wolves manager Ron Allen was quoted in one newspaper as saying it was the most fantastic match he had ever seen.

This was the climax of an eventful and controversial season when promoters thought they could establish soccer in the United States. Their hopes were based on American interest when the 1966 World Cup Finals were televised. Indeed, a game between Santos (Brazil) and Inter-Milan (Italy) brought 41,598 spectators to New York's Yankee Stadium in September 1966.

In 1967 there were two rival leagues operating in the United States. The outlawed National Professional Soccer League (NPSL) had ten clubs, each importing players from a variety of countries. Philadelphia needed to employ a full-time interpreter, while spectators were asked to support strangers, some with names which looked better suited to a optician's eye-chart.

One month into the season the NPSL was averaging only 5,000 spectators per game and was having problems with television coverage. In order to guarantee bursts of advertising every few minutes, the games needed unnatural breaks. Referees were accused of faking fouls to generate a necessary stoppage.

The United Soccer Association, which cunningly abbreviated to USA, was the more successful league. A dozen established clubs, invited from South America and Europe, were asked to pose under American names. They played in two sections (East and West) and the Championship decider would see the two section leaders meet. This is how Aberdeen (sorry, Washington Whips) came to play Wolves (Los Angeles Wolves) in the Memorial Coliseum Stadium on 14 July.

The USA season had not been without its problems. The game between Detroit Cougars (Glentoran of Northern Ireland) and Houston Stars (Bangu of Brazil) was abandoned after 73 minutes as players and spectators fought on the field. And when the New York Skyliners (Cerro of Uruguay) played the Cleveland Stokers (Stoke City of England) police were called in to separate brawling players. Fortunately, the Championship decider would be remembered for its entertainment value.

Wolves and Aberdeen had already met in a mini-league fixture. After a 1–1 draw, an Aberdeen protest was upheld – Wolves manager Ronnie Allen had used three outfield substitutes whereas the rules stated two plus a goalkeeper – and the Scottish club won the replay 3–0. This game could not be taken as a form guide as Wolves players were probably hung-over from their success in winning the Western Division. No one could have predicted the events of the East-West Championship decider.

Peter Knowles (Wolves) and Jim Smith (Aberdeen) scored early goals, but it was not until an hour's play that the game erupted. During a dramatic four-minute period, David Burnside of Wolves twice scored equalizers, cancelling out goals by Frank Munro and Jim Storrie.

When Aberdeen's Jim Smith was sent off in the 80th minute, and then David Burnside put Wolves ahead, the game looked lost for Aberdeen. But Frank Munro made it 4–4 with a last-minute penalty. Extra-time was necessary.

Derek Dougan gave Wolves a 5–4 lead and again Aberdeen looked a beaten team, expecially when Terry Wharton stepped up to take a Wolves penalty with only a few minutes to play. Goalkeeper Bobby Clark saved the penalty, Aberdeen won their own penalty, and, for the second time in the match, Frank Munro scored a last-minute equalizer. At 5–5, the rules called for sudden-death overtime. The first team to score would win.

The winning goal came in the 126th minute. British reporters referred to it as an own-goal, but the *New York Times* was more gracious, assigning the term 'accidental goal'. Wolves full-back Bobby Thomson escaped down the left wing, his cross deceived Clark and the ball bounced off Ally Shewin's thigh into the open goal. The crowd was stunned for a moment, then they realized that Wolves had won. The Championship was theirs, although Ronnie Allen sportingly suggested that the fairest thing after such a game would be to chop the trophy in half. They should award trophies for strangeness.

A TOUCH OF MAYHEM

MONTEVIDEO, NOVEMBER 1967

Celtic, European Cup holders, played Racing Club of Argentina, South America Cup winners, for the championship of the world. Celtic won 1–0 in Glasgow, Racing won 2–1 in Buenos Aires. The play-off was in Uruguay.

Some people suspected there would be trouble. Before the game in Buenos Aires, Celtic goalkeeper Ronnie Simpson was hit on the head by a missile, and John Fallon was hastily substituted. Tension had been building up, and, when the play-off started, referee Rodolfo Perez Oserio from Paraguay soon knew it would be one of his most difficult games. In the 25th minute he called together the two captains and issued a warning.

One man receiving plenty of rough treatment was Celtic winger Jimmy Johnstone, a tiny, jinking player, whose natural game was to take on defenders in tight spaces. In the 37th minute Johnstone was fouled by Rulli, and Celtic players rushed in to protect their winger. Fights broke out and next it was the police's turn to rush in and do some protecting.

After a five-minute delay, Basile (Racing) and Lennox (Celtic) were sent off. The brawl continued with ten aside. By half-time Celtic had conceded 24 fouls and Racing ten.

In the 48th minute, Jimmy Johnstone, fouled yet again, retaliated by hitting Martin. Johnstone was sent off, Celtic were a man short and, eight minutes later, Cardenas scored for Racing, the first goal of the game.

138

John Hughes was the next to go, sent off for a blatant foul on the Racing goalkeeper. Celtic's chances of saving the game seemed to have completely disappeared, although Racing's Rulli was sent off with four minutes to play. That left eight Celtic players against nine of Racing.

With two minutes to play another free-for-all broke out, and it was a wonder the game was ever finished. The referee implied he had sent off Celtic's Bertie Auld, but the Celtic man was still on the field at the end. By then there was nothing but confusion. And television coverage, claimed by some to be ghoulish, added to the debacle. Never before had so many players been sent off in a game involving a professional British team.

THE REFEREE'S WINNING GOAL

BARROW, NOVEMBER 1968

Barrow 0 Plymouth Argyle 0. Thirteen minutes to play. Then came a goal to settle this Division Three game, scored by the most unlikely person on the pitch – referee Ivan Robinson.

Barrow won a corner-kick. The ball was cleared out. George McLean shot hard from outside the penalty area and the ball was going well wide. Referee Robinson, perhaps 15 yards from goal, was in the ball's path. He jumped up to avoid the ball but it hit him on the inside of his left foot and flew off at an angle. Plymouth goalkeeper Pat Dunne was completely deceived by the deflection. Having moved to cover McLean's shot, Dunne was stranded as the ball shot past him into the net. Barrow 1 (The Referee) Plymouth 0.

The rules are quite clear. The ball is in play if it rebounds off either the referee or linesmen when they are in the field of play. Ivan Robinson knew that. He pointed meekly to the centre-circle to confirm his goal. Plymouth players looked stunned and shocked.

The incident spurred Plymouth into a frenzied late rally. Barrow hung on to win 1–0 and the referee had to try to avoid congratulatory pats on the back from Barrow supporters as he ran off the field.

Barrow took their unbeaten home run to 18 games and moved into second place in Division Three, probably

140

the highest position they ever reached in the Football League. Diplomatically, they credited the goal to McLean.

Plymouth were left with a long, disconsolate journey home, hardly assuaged by Mr Robinson's subsequent apology.

THE SOCCER WAR

MEXICO CITY, JUNE 1969

At stake was a place in the 1970 World Cup Finals. Two
Latin American countries, Honduras and El Salvador, were
to play off, home and away, and the winners would meet
Haiti to contest one of sixteen places available at Mexico's
first World Cup Finals. The outcome of the Honduras-El
Salvador confrontation was later dubbed the 'soccer war'.

Antagonism between Honduras and El Salvador had
actually been smouldering for ten years or more. The
countries had serious internal problems – over-population,
poverty and dependence upon simple agricultural economies.
By spring 1969 about 300,000 Salvadorans were living in the
much larger bordering country of Honduras. Their presence
began to be resented, and land-reform laws were introduced
to deprive them of farms. On 30 April they were given thirty
days to leave their land.

The mood can be gauged by some of the mud that was slung
across the border in May. The Honduran Minister of Foreign
Affairs linked Colgate toothpaste (made in El Salvador) to an
increased incidence of cavities among Honduran children. El
Salvador authorities alleged that Glostora haircream (made
in Honduras) caused dandruff. By June, the month of the
soccer games, tension was running exceedingly high.

Honduras were at home first. The Salvadorans stayed at
the Hotel Prado in Tegucigalpa, where they were 'serenaded'
all night by whistles, fireworks and shouting. The next day,

in the bowl-like stadium at the base of a hill which sported a classical Peace Monument, El Salvador lost 1–0.

A week later came the return game in San Salvador. An El Salvador win would bring a play-off as the competition was on a points rather than goals basis. The Honduras players, not surprisingly, were treated to a reciprocal serenade the night before this return game. Many Hondurans who had travelled to San Salvador caught the hostile mood and decided to watch the game on television instead of attending the Flor Blanca stadium. When they witnessed the stone-throwing and water-bombing they must have been glad to have stayed at home. Furthermore, the game was one-sided. Two goals from Martinez (one a penalty) and one from Acevedo gave El Salvador a 3–0 lead at half-time. There was no second-half scoring but it was now one game each. A play-off was necessary.

Only two Honduran supporters were seriously injured but this was enough to cause outrage in local newspaper columns. The day after the game paramilitary groups in Honduras forcibly evicted Salvadoran peasants from lands they had farmed for years. Tens of thousands of Salvadorans flocked over the border, back to their already over-populated native country.

On 26 June El Salvador broke off diplomatic relations with Honduras. Three days later came the World Cup qualifying play-off. Fortunately, cool heads had suggested a neutral venue. The game was staged at the Aztec Stadium, Mexico City, and about 1,700 Mexican policemen were assigned to duty.

In the circumstances the game was surprisingly peaceful. True, there was one outburst of '*asesinos, asesinos*' ('murderers, murderers') from the El Salvador fans, but the fear of feuding among the crowd (about 15,000) proved unfounded, even when the game went into extra-time. The winning goal fell to El Salvador, who recorded a 3–2 victory. Martinez again scored twice.

Early in July Honduran and Salvadoran troops crossed the border. Honduras bragged it had the region's best air-force,

143

but, on 14 July, it was El Salvador who made a crucial aerial attack – on the airport at Tegucigalpa. This precipitated the so-called 'soccer war'. The war lasted four days, until economic sanctions by the Organization of American States (OAS) forced El Salvador to withdraw with a psychological victory.

Those people who have studied the war, such as Thomas Anderson in *The War of the Dispossessed* and Robert Armstrong and Janet Shenk in *Salvador: The Face of Revolution*, have shown that it was caused by problematic relationships between peasants and landowners, soldiers and civilians, trade-unionists and employers, and was not over anything as 'trivial' as soccer. However, it was certainly one of the strangest political contexts in which a soccer game has occurred.

Nor was that all for the winners, whose progress towards the 1970 World Cup Finals continued to be very odd. After a sound 2–1 win in Haiti, El Salvador might have left reasonably confident. All they required was a draw at home. But Haiti brought along a witch-doctor. He sprinkled some powder on the field, chanted a spell and Haiti were three up at half-time.

The two countries travelled to Kingston, Jamaica, for a closely contested play-off. The game's first goal didn't arrive until extra time, when Martinez scored for El Salvador. Then El Salvador's Argentinian coach Gregorio Bundio took one of the strangest tactical decisions of his career – he punched the witch-doctor and put him out of the game. El Salvador won 1–0.

Bundio had coached El Salvador through ten World Cup qualifying games (including two which went to extra-time), a war and the threat of a witch-doctor. However, he was dismissed from his job before the Mexico Finals, caught up in a dispute between the players and their government. The players felt they were owed money promised for reaching the Finals. The government said the money would have to go towards the costs of the war the players had helped to cause.

In Mexico, El Salvador lost three games – 3–0 to Belgium, 4–0 to Mexico and 2–0 to Russia. They held out for 44 minutes against the hosts, Mexico, and then a disputed goal provoked uproar, threatening to end the match. Eventually the Egyptian referee found an ideal solution – he blew for half-time – and the crowd were left to contemplate the chances of war in the second half.

SOUTH AMERICAN FREE-FOR-ALL

BUENOS AIRES, MARCH 1971

It happened in the closing minutes of a South American (Libertadores) Cup match. Argentinian champions Boca Juniors and Sporting Cristal of Peru were locked at two goals apiece, and 65,000 were watching the contest in Boca's Bombonera ('Chocolate Box') Stadium. Neither side had much chance to qualify from the four-team group, but when Ruben Zune, the Boca Juniors' captain, was tackled and toppled over, he saw red. First he saw his blood. Next he felt his own anger. He attacked his assailant, and then it started.

The scene was what United States ice-hockey followers would call a bench-emptying brawl. Officials, coaches, reserves and almost all the players joined in. Referee Alejandro Otero could do little on his own except stand and observe 19 players commit sending-off offences. He called in the police.

By the end of the fracas three players were injured. Zune's cut would need seven stitches. One Peruvian, Mellan, was carried from the field on a stretcher suffering from a fractured skull. Another, Campos, had a broken nose.

Three players – the two goalkeepers and Boca's Peruvian centre-half Menendez – had steered clear of the rumpus, but the other 19 were arrested by the police. The 16 uninjured players were taken to the police station and given a 30-day jail sentence.

There was real danger of the footballers sewing mailbags in shirts of different stripes with different numbers, but diplomats intervened swiftly. The sentences were suspended. Yet it was six weeks before all the Boca players had served their playing suspensions. Boca, the biggest club in Argentina, had reserves but not of the same standard.

This was another sad episode in the Libertadores Cup, the competition which feeds into the World Club Championship by pitting its winners against the European Cup holders. Originally the Champion Clubs Cup, it had already staged a 3½-hour marathon between Penarol and Santos in 1962 – the Chilean referee twice suspended the game when officials were hit by missiles from the crowd – and there were allegations in 1966 that River Plate's two Uruguayans had sold the Argentinian club down its own river. Not to mention a 1970 Nacional-Penarol eruption which was almost on the same scale as the game which saw 19 players sent off. Almost, but not quite.

THE VITAL DISPUTED GOAL

LEEDS, APRIL 1971

If soccer historians needed to choose one game as a watershed of soccer's modern era, then the Leeds-West Brom game of 1970–1 would be a strong candidate: winning was the sole objective for one team, the play was a hallmark of professionalism and gamesmanship, the referee's decisions were challenged, the crowd invaded the pitch and there was an early example of trial by television.

Don Revie's Leeds United were desperate to turn their success into more tangible honours. After winning the Second Division in 1964, they had won the League Championship once, the League Cup once and the Inter-Cities Fairs Cup once; but they also had a remarkable record of frustration – second in the League on three occasions, twice beaten FA Cup Finalists, twice beaten in FA Cup semi-finals, beaten by Celtic in a European Cup semi-final, beaten finalists in the Inter-Cities Fairs Cup and semi-finalists in another Fairs Cup year.

Now, as they raced neck and neck with Arsenal, came another excellent chance for the League Championship. Early exits from the League Cup and FA Cup – the latter an embarrassing defeat at Fourth Division Colchester United – left the League as Leeds' last hope of success in the 1970–1 season. They had four games to play. Their visitors on 17 April, West Bromwich Albion, were unlikely to stand in their way. West Brom hadn't won an away game for 16 months.

148

Nevertheless, West Brom were a better team than their poor League position and recent away results indicated. Centre-backs John Wile and John Kaye contained Leeds strikers Allan Clarke and Mick Jones with the help of offside tactics. Bobby Hope and the young Asa Hartford buzzed in midfield. And, after a mistake by Jack Charlton, Jeff Astle and Colin Suggett set up a 15th-minute goal for Tony Brown. At half-time West Brom led Leeds United 1–0.

According to Leeds supporters, the worst team on the pitch were the officials. They noted the name of referee Ray Tinkler, a company secretary from Lincolnshire, and linesman Colin Cartlich from Hull when they combined to rule Mick Jones offside when he put the ball into the West Brom net. Then, in the 69th minute, came the incident which pitched referee Tinkler into the national limelight.

Norman Hunter, Leeds' English international defender, played a careless pass. The ball bounced off Albion's Tony Brown and into space on the Leeds left flank. Brown took up the challenge and started a run for goal. His team-mate Colin Suggett was ten yards further on, in a more central position, discreetly heading in the opposite direction to Brown . . . but not discreetly enough. Suggett was spotted by linesman Troupe (South Shields), who raised his flag. Leeds midfielder Mick Bates appealed from the halfway-line. Tony Brown hesitated. Referee Tinkler raised his whistle towards his mouth, and then he thought again.

Consider the referee's position. There was no doubt that Suggett was in an offside position, but was he interfering with play or seeking to gain an advantage? Certainly the Leeds players thought he was, and that was enough to affect the play. Some people refused to accept the idea that a player might not be interfering with play, claiming that all players should be interfering with play throughout the game, for we were now on the verge of the concept of 'total football'. The law was clear. The referee had discretion to decide.

Confusion was caused by the linesman's role. His raised flag was informing the tall, balding Tinkler that a player was in an offside position. The referee would decide if the player

149

was interfering with play. But some referees also asked the linesmen to decide before raising their flags.

Referee Ray Tinkler waved play on. Tony Brown continued his run, honing in on the near post. Brown passed the ball across the face of Gary Sprake's goal. It was tapped into the net by Jeff Astle, who might have been in an offside position but the linesman wasn't in the best position to see. Tinkler gave a goal.

The entire Leeds team surrounded the referee. About 20 spectators ran on to the field and police closed them down. Players protected the referee, but the linesman at the other end, Colin Cartlich, was hit by a can and needed treatment from Leeds trainer Les Cocker.

It was some time before order was restored and the game resumed. Albion now led 2–0, and Leeds' Championship hopes were receding. Although Allan Clarke pulled back a goal, Leeds lost 2–1. Sixteen days later Arsenal won the Championship by a point.

The outcry from Leeds officials after the game was as provocative as that of the spectators. Manager Don Revie called for full-time referees and said that nine months' work had been ruined by one man (meaning Tinkler). Chairman Percy Woodward was even more outspoken, almost supporting the actions of the pitch invaders. Leeds United were later fined £750 and Elland Road was closed for the first four home matches of the next season.

These events may not seem strange by today's standards. But at the time they certainly were. Yet it was only soccer history's curious knack of repeating itself. Back in 1912 West Brom had won 1–0 at Leeds City in an FA Cup tie, and Leeds supporters greeted the only goal with claims of handball, offside and that the ball went through a hole in the net. Leeds manager Scott Walford had to plead with hundreds of spectators before they went home.

The difference, of course, between 1912 and 1971 was television, which prompted *national* debate. Martin Tyler, in his book *The Story of Football*, described Astle's goal as the most disputed goal of the 1970s.

THE HIGH-SCORERS' CUP FINAL

WEST BROMWICH, AUGUST 1971

The Watney Cup, an early sponsored tournament, was designed for high-scoring teams, not that there were many about in the early 1970s. West Brom (68 goals scored in the First Division in 1970–1) and Colchester United (70 goals in Division Four) were among the qualifiers. Their Watney Cup Final, played at the end of the eight-team pre-season tournament, justified their selection. Under an experimental offside law, the game had plenty of goals, a penalty-kick competition and an unusual result.

Don Howe had just taken over as West Brom manager. A former West Brom, Arsenal and England player, he was fresh from success as coach to the Arsenal double-winning team. People were predicting a stronger defence than under previous manager Alan Ashman.

Colchester United manager Dick Graham also had West Brom connections – he had been trainer and coach under Vic Buckingham – but had enjoyed a less illustrious playing career than Howe, as a goalkeeper with Leicester City, Northampton Town and Crystal Palace. As a manager he was one of the original gimmick men, shuffling players' shirts at Crystal Palace – the centre-half will wear number seven, and so on – and turning the dressing-room into a relaxing lounge. At Colchester he produced a super-fit team and promised to scale the walls of Colchester Castle if they beat Leeds United in the FA Cup. They won 3–2.

An experimental offside law meant players could only be offside inside the penalty area. At half-time West Brom led 3–2 with goals by Len Cantello, Jeff Astle and Colin Suggett. Mick Mahon and David Simmons scored for Colchester.

Mahon equalized in the 65th minute and Colchester looked to have won the game when Brian Lewis scored an 88th-minute penalty. But Astle equalized. Four-four.

The game went to penalty-kicks. West Brom shot first. They scored three out of the first four and needed the fifth to stay in the game as Colchester had scored their first four. Len Cantello shot over the crossbar and Fourth Division Colchester won with a penalty in hand.

THE ENDLESS CUP-TIE

ALVECHURCH, OXFORD AND BIRMINGHAM, NOVEMBER 1971

When Alvechurch of the Midland Combination and Oxford City of the Isthmian League played out their final qualifying round FA Cup-tie, people began to joke that the Cup Final might have to be delayed. It took six games and 660 playing minutes to decide the tie. Finally, Bobby Hope's 588th-minute headed goal divided the teams and champagne flowed in both dressing-rooms.

The marathon started and finished on treacherous pitches. The Cup-tie moved from Alvechurch's Lye Meadow (with its corner-to-corner slope) to Aston Villa's Villa Park, calling on the way at Oxford City's White House, Birmingham City's St Andrews and Oxford United's Manor Stadium (where two games were played).

At Alvechurch, the home team led 2–0 but Oxford clawed back into the game to force the first draw. Had Oxford City goalkeeper Peter Harris not dived bravely at the feet of Bobby Hope (not the Scottish international) late in the game, a lot of travelling might have been avoided.

The Cup-tie was chronicled excellently by *Oxford Mail* reporter Jim Rosenthal, who covered five of the six games. His only mistake was to suggest that Alvechurch might have missed their best chance. 'In this competition,' Rosenthal wrote, 'You only get one bite at the cherry, and Oxford will

153

want to emphasize that point at the White House tomorrow night.'

In fact, Alvechurch had another five bites at the cherry, something neither Rosenthal nor anyone else could have predicted. By the time of the first replay, the two teams knew the winners would play Aldershot (away) in the first round of the FA Cup proper. Aldershot manager Jimmy Melia turned up to watch his future opponents without realizing that he would have four more opportunities to see them play. By the end of the saga Melia might have considered how best to use his time.

The first replay, the most rugged of the six games, had two first-half goals, shared of course. By the end of extra-time the two teams were exhausted, but Alvechurch maintained their season's unbeaten away record.

The next game was in Birmingham – almost a home game for Alvechurch – and the 3,600 crowd was the highest attendance of the six. Having drawn a league game on the Saturday, Oxford City extended their sequence with an equalizer just after half-time of this second replay. But that was the last goal the Cup-tie produced for about 330 minutes.

There was enough action. Another fine save from Harris (after 324 minutes) kept the third match alive, while City's Andy Mitchell cleared from the goal-line (365 minutes) and Tommy Eales twice hit the crossbar (388 minutes and 449 minutes) in the goalless fourth game.

It became an endurance test. Alvechurch midfielder Derek Davis, a car-worker on nights, had to be rested from the fourth game. City's Eric Metcalfe, a schoolteacher, received a hairline fibula fracture in the fifth game. The trainers became experts on cramp.

The *Oxford Mail*'s Bill Beckett, deputizing for Jim Rosenthal at the fourth game, reported that someone in the crowd suggested an annual reunion for those who had thus far watched all four games. Unfortunately, a few minutes after the fifth game (one of three in Oxford), an elderly Alvechurch supporter collapsed and died.

By the sixth game, at Villa Park, there was little new

for coaches John Fisher (Oxford City) and Rhys Davies (Alvechurch) to try. The two teams knew each other very well. Fisher was forced to make changes, however, as the Army couldn't release two of his men and two other key players were injured. Then came Bobby Hope's goal in the 18th minute of the sixth game. The winners were Alvechurch.

For the record, the six games were as follows:

Sat. 6 Nov. (Alvechurch) Alvechurch 2 (Horne, Allner), Oxford City 2 (McCrae, Metcalfe)

Tues. 9 Nov. (Oxford) Oxford City 1 (Eales) Alvechurch 1 (Allner)

Mon. 15 Nov. (Birmingham) Alvechurch 1 (Allner) Oxford City 1 (Goucher)

Wed. 17 Nov. (Oxford) Alvechurch 0 Oxford City 0

Sat. 20 Nov. (Oxford) Alvechurch 0 Oxford City 0

Mon. 22 Nov. (Villa Park) Alvechurch 1 (Hope) Oxford City 0

(All except the first and last went to extra-time.)

The first round game against Aldershot was delayed, but only by four days. Alvechurch, playing their ninth game in 18 days, went down 4–2 and were out of the competition.

When the draw for the FA Amateur Cup was made a week later you can almost imagine a wag going into the Oxford City dressing-room: 'Heard the draw, lads? Alvechurch away.' Fortunately, it didn't happen.

REFEREE WHO FORGOT THE RULES

LISBON, NOVEMBER 1971

One of the most embarrassing refereeing errors of recent years came when Dutchman van Ravens got the rules wrong during the second leg of a second-round European Cup-winners' Cup tie between Sporting Lisbon and Glasgow Rangers.

All referees make mistakes occasionally. Such errors usually result from the officials' inability to see everything from every angle and make the correct split-second decision. This gives rise to a spate of jokes and stories about 'blindness' ('I agreed to escort the referee to the railway station,' said the policeman, 'because I always like to take care of the handicapped') and 'bias' ('We were playing against twelve men'). Those familiar with refereeing history are probably aware that many contemporary referees are often compared with the much-respected official in the 1878 FA Cup Final, Mr Segar Bastard.

Most major refereeing howlers occurred in the early days of soccer. There was the referee who ordered off a dumb man for abusive language (the decision was later reversed), the referee who headed a goal (he apologized but had to let the goal stand) and the referee who stood in a dressing-room washbowl and broke it.

In the post-war era a referee at Sunderland in 1954 started the second half before realizing that only one linesman was

156

in place. In front of 43,000 people, his face was as red as the missing flag.

At Wimbledon, in 1983, a referee wrongly awarded Millwall a goal after Wimbledon full-back Wally Downes chipped a direct free-kick over goalkeeper Dave Beasant's head and into his own net. The correct decision here is a corner-kick; the early rule-makers sensibly decided that a team scoring in its own net from a direct free-kick shouldn't be punished more heavily than if it had done so from an indirect free-kick, as the offence being punished was obviously more serious in the first instance.

Refereeing can give rise to all manner of wild questions about soccer oddities and offbeat features of the game. For example, a penalty kick is taken, the ball bursts as it is kicked, the casing flies over the crossbar, the lace spins out and wraps itself around the goalkeeper's neck, hindering him from saving the bladder as it sails into the net – what is the correct decision?

That incident, as far as I am aware, never happened, even in the days when balls had laces. But the events in Lisbon in 1971 showed that one referee had not been tested on the rules of the competition.

Raangers had won the first leg at Ibrox Park 3–2, after being 2–0 ahead at one stage. Now they had a difficult game in Lisbon. Sporting Lisbon twice took the lead. Each time Colin Stein equalized. Then Rangers' Scottish international centre-half Ron McKinnon fractured a leg, and Sporting took the lead again with 25 minutes to play. Somehow Rangers hung on to take the tie into extra-time.

During this period both teams scored once. Thereupon, referee van Ravens ordered each team to take five penalties to decide the tie. Rangers qualified for some sort of record by missing all five kicks. In fact, Tommy McLean missed twice as the Sporting goalkeeper moved too quickly for the first. Sporting won 3–0 on penalties and were through to the next round. Or were they?'

The Scottish journalists were already scratching their heads in bewilderment. Surely, they thought, away goals count double in the event of a tie. At the end of extra-time Rangers had scored *three* away goals against Sporting's *two* in Glasgow.

The referee was wrong. Rangers were indeed the winners. The UEFA officials later reversed the referee's decision and suspended the Dutch referee. The rules were very clear. The provision that away goals counted double in the event of a draw also applied to those scored in extra-time. That gave rise to an even better sporting question: which team missed all its six penalties during a penalty shoot-out and still won the tie?

That season Glasgow Rangers won the European Cup-winners' Cup.

SIXTEEN MINUTES OF DISBELIEF

BIRKENHEAD, MARCH 1972

A strange match creates a crowd atmosphere, a prevailing group mood of anger, laughter, shock or sheer bewilderment, depending on the events concerned. Sometimes, when a match gaily runs completely out of control, spectators turn to neighbours for confirmation of what they are seeing.

That happened to me the night Tranmere Rovers played Walsall. I experienced 16 minutes of disbelief.

It was my second season of supporting Rovers. I had cheered them through their glorious record-breaking season of 1970–1 – no team had ever drawn as many as 22 League games before – and now watched in awe as they blazed a trail towards the Division Three relegation zone. Most Rovers home games were on Friday evenings in those days, the crowd swollen by Liverpool or Everton fans taking a night off from the Anfield Kop or Gladys Street end.

Liverpool fans were particularly enticed in 1971–2, when Tranmere signed Liverpool internationals Ron 'Rowdy' Yeats, soon to become Rovers' manager, and Tommy Lawrence, a goalkeeper affectionately known by the Kop as the 'Fat Cat' or 'Flying Pig'. Lawrence was a roly-poly goalie, small and podgy, deceptively agile, fearless and cumbersome enough to make it very awkward for forwards when he narrowed their shooting angles.

By the time he joined Tranmere, Lawrence was well past his Scottish international peak, slower and heavier, and looking even less like an athlete. I remember one incident when he waddled and grovelled endlessly along the goal-line to collect a stray back-pass near the corner of his penalty area. With no one remotely near him, he stopped the ball with his body, knocked it out of the penalty area, trod on it, picked himself up, dragged the ball back into the penalty area and stood, eventually, clutching his treasure. The crowd had been deathly quiet. Then one spectator spoke clearly and loudly in unsolicited admiration. 'All I saw was a green blur,' he said.

By the end of March 1972, Rovers were still drawing games but not crowds. 'If they played in our backyard I'd draw the curtains,' I remember someone saying at the end of one game. There were just 2,320 present the Monday night Walsall visited.

Occupants of the press-box must have been grateful when news of the attendance reached them in the second half. They could add a comment on Rovers' lowest attendance of the season – in fact it was one of the five lowest in the Division that season – to the meagre notes they already had: drab and goalless . . . both sides failed to control the ball in the wind . . . Tranmere's slump continued . . . Rovers badly missed injured assistant manager Ron Yeats . . . no sign of a goal . . . Chic Brodie showed some neat touches in midfield . . . Rovers failed to take advantage of the gale at their backs in the first half . . . after 62 minutes Adrian Maher came on as substitute for ex-Walsall centre-forward John Manning . . . neither goalkeeper had a save to make . . .

I entertained myself by walking around the terraces, until I was behind Tommy Lawrence's goal, totally alone in that section of the ground. A bitter, biting wind tore through my clothing. In front of me, Lawrence stalked his penalty area to keep warm. I thought about the 20,000 Anfield Kop. Here, at Prenton Park, I was on my own, and it was too cold to stay.

I was on my way home, having just reached the Shed, when the game woke up and went crazy.

A free-kick to Walsall and Mick Evans thunders it noisily against the post and Walsall come again, Chris Jones to

Bobby Shinton, whose shot wiggles in the wind with Tommy Lawrence wondering where it went and the game's been given a goal, so Rovers must attack, which they do, Trevor Storton shooting and Stan Jones deflecting the ball up and over Bob Wesson for an own-goal equalizer, and now the action's back to Tommy Lawrence who knocks down Colin Harrison's shot for Geoff Morris to score another for Walsall and there's nobody on the 'Kop' to see it from close quarters, or to strain their eyes as Wesson makes a great save at the other end and another and another but he can't reach Storton's cross and Maher scores another equalizer so Walsall come straight down and Bobby Shinton topples over Syd Farrimond's legs and Harrison hits the penalty past Lawrence for the third Walsall goal and Rovers have hardly any time left when Maher puts over a corner-kick and Storton lunges and it's Rovers' third equalizer in about ten minutes and the game ends and we can breathe again.

Three-three in 16 minutes. Had it been like that all through the game it would have finished 17 apiece. I have seen games lurch out of control on many other occasions, but never to that extent and never after 74 minutes of tedium. Football, at times, thoroughly rewards the patience of people at places like Prenton Park. That season Tranmere Rovers escaped relegation on goal average.

CROWD POWER

NEWCASTLE, MARCH 1974

Should the Newcastle United–Nottingham Forest FA Cup tie
have been abandoned after 55 minutes and the result allowed
to stand? If so, Forest would have won 3–1 and gained a place
in the semi-final. Instead it took five hours of playing time
and many more hours spent in meetings before the outcome
was settled. The eventual winners were Newcastle United.

On form, Second Division Forest were given little chance
against First Division United, but St James's Park was a likely
place for an FA Cup upset. That season Newcastle had twice
been held to shock home draws – by non-League Hendon and
Fourth Division Scunthorpe United – while two years earlier
non-League Hereford United had done the same and then
beaten Newcastle at Edgar Street.

Goals by Ian Bowyer and Liam O'Kane gave Forest a 2–1
lead at half-time. Then the eruption came in the 55th minute.
David Craig fouled Duncan McKenzie and referee Gordon
Kew gave Forest a penalty-kick. Newcastle centre-half Pat
Howard argued so much that he was sent off. George Lyall
scored the penalty and United, trailing 3–1 on goals and
11–10 down on men, looked a doomed side. A small section
of the crowd changed all that.

According to police estimates, between 300 and 500 spectators took part in the pitch invasion. They spilled on to the
pitch and charged. Two Forest players were assaulted, so
the referee took the players to the dressing-rooms for safety.

162

Twenty-three people were taken to hospital and 103 others treated on the ground. The police made 39 arrests and took eight minutes to clear the pitch.

The teams returned and the game continued, but Forest had lost their initiative. Newcastle surged forward with the bulk of the 54,000 crowd in support. Intimidated, Forest conceded three goals in the last 20 minutes – a penalty by Terry McDermott, a flying header by John Tudor and a volley by Bobby Moncur. One neutral observer said he thought Moncur looked offside but with the crowd in that mood the linesman dared not raise his flag – he would have been lynched.

A special FA commission concluded that the 4–3 Newcastle victory was achieved in a hostile environment. Even though Newcastle had already been drawn against Burnley in the semi-final, the result of their sixth-round game was annulled. The FA ordered the match to be replayed on neutral ground, a decision which infuriated Newcastle officials and players. 'My reaction is one of disgust, but not surprise,' said centre-forward Malcolm MacDonald. 'I half-expected a ridiculous solution, and they came up with one.'

It took two games to reach a decision. The teams drew 0–0 (after extra-time) at Goodison Park on Monday 18 March, and, three days later, at the same venue, Malcolm MacDonald scored the only goal of the game. That season Newcastle reached the FA Cup Final, losing to Liverpool, while people pondered on the long-term implications of that March day at St James's Park. If a partisan crowd was worth a goal start, then a pitch invasion could be worth three.

THE POLICE OPEN FIRE

ADDIS ABABA, ETHIOPIA, MAY 1974

The Kenyan party were apprehensive about the trip to Ethiopia. Although Abaluhya led Asmara 2–0 from the first leg of their African Club Championship tie, there was a feeling that something could go wrong. Two goals seemed adequate security to win the game. They were more worried about other kinds of security. There was some relief when the game was switched from Asmara's home ground to the Haile Selassie national stadium, where security was likely to be better.

Abaluhya coach Dan Anyanzwa still remembered the Ethiopia-Kenya game in 1970, when, as a member of the Kenya team, he had seen nine team-mates hurt in the crowd rumpus which caused the game's abandonment after 55 minutes. Old-timers recalled the 1963 Ethiopia-Kenya international which had also been volatile.

The 1974 Asmara-Abaluhya second leg lasted until the 83rd minute. Asmara led 1–0, the goal scored, according to Kenyan accounts, when Abaluhya players were dodging stones and bottles thrown by the crowd. The police had already intervened to quell one on-the-pitch tussle. Now they came in with a vengeance. As referee Punda of Zaire abandoned the game, the police opened fire. At least two people were killed.

Several players were injured, none of them seriously. The Kenyan team were driven from the ground in police

164

cars. They were thankful to be safe in their hotel, even more thankful to return safely to Kenya. None of them would relish the next occasion they were drawn against an Ethiopian team.

UNDER THE SPELL

LONDON, APRIL 1975

I well remember a Saturday in the 1970s when I turned up to watch New Brighton lose a Cheshire League game. New Brighton, losing consistently at the time, were playing the top of the league. Imagine how stunned I was when the Rakers – our affectionate term for the New Brighton lads – went delirious with energy and scored three times in the first half-hour. 'There's been annippnotist in dressing-room,' I was informed by a nearby spectator, who obviously saw how pale I looked. But New Brighton's major tactical defect, I discovered later, was not to call in the hypnotist at half-time. A tired New Brighton team played a more predictable second half and were pegged back to 3–3.

In recent times, hypnotists have become more accepted as a means to relax players and inspire confidence. Ronald Markham, who was known as Romark on the stage, worked with Millwall when they were promoted to Division Two in 1976, and with Halifax Town when, as a Fourth Division team in 1980, they beat First Division Manchester City 1–0 in the FA Cup.

One particular match worth featuring was Tottenham Hotspur's contest with Leeds United at the end of the 1974–5 First Division season. A Spurs defeat would mean relegation to the Second Division. Terry Neill, Spurs' manager, called in Ronald Markham, who hypnotized the team before the game, concentrating on three players – Alfie Conn, Cyril

Knowles and Martin Chivers, who was back in the first team after an absence of two months.

Cyril Knowles had been suffering with a knee injury for more than a year. Markham asked him to talk through a goal he had once scored from a free-kick. The response, during the game, was almost instantaneous. Inside a few minutes Spurs had a free-kick just outside the penalty area. Knowles took it and scored.

Chivers scored a second for Tottenham in the 50th minute, and Knowles, playing full-back, made it three from a penalty. Although Jordan scored for Leeds, Conn made it 4–1 in the 75th minute. The final score was 4–2 and Spurs stayed in the First Division for another two seasons.

THE 28-PENALTY SHOOT-OUT

HONG KONG, JUNE 1975

The Asia Cup semi-final between North Korea and Hong Kong finished 2–2 after 90 minutes and 3–3 after extra-time. The ensuing penalty shoot-out had spectators wondering whether it might have been quicker to play another game.

It was an agonizing few hours for North Korea coach Pak Du-ik, best remembered in Britain for the goal that beat Italy in the 1966 World Cup Finals. His team led by two goals in the game against Hong Kong, then looked in danger of losing 3–2 when Hong Kong scored with seven minutes of extra-time remaining. The penalty shoot-out tested the coach's nerve even more.

Hong Kong took the first penalty and scored. North Korea took the second penalty and scored. Hong Kong took the next and missed. North Korea missed their second too, and then the neck-and-neck competition continued.

Each team scored five of their first six. Lai Sun-cheung took Hong Kong's seventh kick. He missed. It was now 'sudden death'. Up stepped Cha Jung-sok to take North Korea's seventh kick. Hong Kong goalkeeper Chu Kwok-kuen saved it.

It was back to stalemate, each team scoring with alternate kicks. Soon, all the players except the goal-keepers had taken kicks, and they had to start over again.

Wu Kwok-hung took Hong Kong's 13th kick and missed.

Pak Jung-hun had the chance to win the game for North Korea but his penalty was saved by Chu Kwok-kuen.

The duel continued.

Hong Kong missed their 14th penalty too, so Kim Jung-min was the next potential match-winner for North Korea. He shot left-footed, low to the goalkeeper's right. Chu Kwok-kuen moved the wrong way and the game was over. North Korea had won the penalty shoot-out 11–10 on the 28th penalty. They were very tired when they beat China in the Asia Cup Final a few days later.

OVATION FOR A STREAKER

PETERBOROUGH, AUGUST 1975

She waited until half-time on the first day of the new season, a day warm enough for what she intended. The teams returned from their break and walked, or trotted, to their places, the players in little huddles, discussing the half-time words of their managers, Noel Cantwell (Peterborough United) and Doug Fraser (Walsall). Then came a distraction.

The teenager with waist-length hair was clad, while on the terraces, in a light-coloured blouse and dark, bell-bottomed trousers. As she ran on to the London Road pitch she peeled off her blouse and undid her bra. The crowd cheered. Not the usual excited cheer for egging on the team during the game – just a light-hearted, good-humoured cheer.

Naked to the waist, she ran around in circles among the players and then set off back towards the terrace. A policeman met her there. He took off his helmet, covered up her bare breasts and led her gently out of the ground. All the crowd shouted good-humoured comments. I won't speculate as to what they were, but the *Peterborough Evening Telegraph*, on the Monday after the game (which finished 0–0), ran a front-page cartoon showing two supporters talking: 'A good afternoon's entertainment, Albert . . . Posh got a point and the streaker had two.'

Yes, there was also a game. Both teams had new signings on show – Miah Dennehy for Walsall and Peter Eustace for

170

Peterborough – and the two goalkeepers, Mick Kearns (Walsall) and Eric Steele (Peterborough), both played well. The dearth of goals gave the papers the chance to say that the streaker earned the biggest cheer of the afternoon, but that was probably stretching the point.

There was also a streaker at Arsenal in 1982, but, so far, no soccer streaker has achieved the prominence of Erica Roe, who, when 24, ran semi-naked on to the Twickenham pitch at half-time of an England–Australia rugby international. Erica Roe chose London rather than London Road, Peterborough, a televised game rather than a Third Division soccer match, a capacity crowd rather than an attendance of 7,174 people. Film of Erica Roe streaking was shown on television news and she was soon offered a job modelling double-breasted jackets.

THE ONE-SCORER FOUR-GOAL DRAW

LEICESTER, MARCH 1976

Northern Ireland international Chris Nicholl, now manager of Southampton, played 648 Football League games during his long career with Halifax Town, Luton Town, Aston Villa, Southampton and Grimsby Town. None was more bizarre than Aston Villa's away game at Leicester City in March 1976, which goes down in history for Nicholl's remarkable piece of goalscoring. The tall central defender scored all four goals in a 2–2 draw. Twice he headed own-goals to put Leicester ahead. Twice he equalized with close-range shots.

The game at Leicester was the 18th of 21 away games Aston Villa failed to win that season, their first season back in Division One. They started well enough, but Leicester went ahead after 15 minutes, Nicholl heading Brian Alderson's shot on to a better course for it to find the net. In the 40th minute, however, after Brian Little's header had created confusion in the Leicester penalty area, Nicholl hooked in an equalizer for Villa.

Eight minutes after half-time Chris Nicholl conceded his second own-goal. Leicester's Frank Worthington lobbed the ball into the penalty area and Nicholl, challenging with Bob Lee, sent another fine header past John Burridge. But, once again, he cancelled out his own-goal with one at the other end. Four minutes were left when 'Chico' Hamilton sent over

172

a corner-kick. A scramble in the goalmouth gave Nicholl a chance to put boot on ball, and there was his fourth goal of the game, his second for Villa.

Chris Nicholl's amazing feat of two for each side equalled the 'achievement' of Sam Wynne in a 1923 game for Oldham Athletic against Manchester United. Wynne scored a free-kick and a penalty-kick for Oldham and two own-goals for Manchester United. Oldham won 3–2. But, in Nicholl's case, all his goals came from open play and they were the *only* goals of the game.

Also, there were a couple of strange indicators from the previous week. Chris Nicholl had scored an own-goal a week before, diverting a shot from Tottenham Hotspur's Ralph Coates past John Burridge. And, on the same day, Leicester had beaten Middlesbrough, the only goal of the game being an own-goal by tall Middlesbrough central defender Stuart Boam.

One of the strangest things about Nicholl's performance was his two goals for Villa. His goals usually came from his head, but here he was scoring with his feet. It was surprising that Villa never used him as an out-and-out attacker. After all, that day at Leicester he demonstrated that he had the one thing that all natural goalscorers possess – a beautiful sense of balance.

THE GAME THAT NEVER WAS

LEATHERHEAD, FEBRUARY 1978

Leatherhead were drawn at home to Dartford in the second round of the FA Trophy. Conditions were not good, but match referee Vickers of Essex declared the pitch fit after an inspection an hour and a half before kick-off. Dartford never turned up.

The Leatherhead players waited, the crowd at Fetcham Grove waited, even the Dartford directors who had travelled under their own steam waited. There was no sign of the Dartford team coach.

There were four differing accounts of why the Dartford coach-driver was told to turn round at Croydon, which was over halfway of a journey of less than 30 miles. Certainly someone made a telephone call from Croydon. One account says a young girl answered and told them the game was postponed. Another says it was the secretary who confirmed the match was off. A third account suggests Dartford were the victims of a hoax. A fourth guess might be that someone dialled the wrong number. If a stranger phoned your house at Saturday lunchtime and came straight to the point – 'Is the game on, Leatherhead?' – you probably wouldn't be stuck for a negative answer.

So, while Dartford players were at home watching the rugby on television, Leatherhead players were put through a stiff training session. Although people at the ground felt Dartford were to blame, no one was fined over the incident.

Dartford were allowed to replay the fixture without punishment. On the following Thursday Leatherhead won 5–1,
Chris Kelly scoring two goals.

The morals of the tale are to ensure that telephones are
staffed responsibly at key times and to seek confirmation of
any news received. These points can be made more forcibly
by reference to a cunning piece of corruption which took
place in 1904. Before an important game between Bristol
East and Warmley, the Bristol East goalkeeper received a
telegram from the Bristol East secretary saying the match
would not take place. Warmley were delighted when Bristol
East were forced to scratch around at the last minute for a
replacement goalkeeper. When it was later learned that the
telegram had been sent by Warmley officials, the Football
Association handed out three suspensions.

WARRING TEAM-MATES

LONDON, JANUARY 1979

There is a clear statement contained in the twelfth of soccer's 17 laws: a player shall be sent off the field of play if, in the opinion of the referee, he is guilty of violent conduct or serious foul play.

This statement does not specify that the violent conduct must be towards an opponent for it to warrant a sending-off punishment. The violence could be directed at a team-mate, although that is extremely rare.

There were five minutes to play in the game at the Valley Stadium. Charlton Athletic and Maidstone United were drawing 1–1 in their FA Cup third-round game. Mike Flanagan, scorer of Charlton's equalizer a few minutes before, played the ball through. Derek Hales, Flanagan's co-striker, was given offside. The bearded Hales was not pleased.

Hales made it clear that he wanted the ball played earlier. Flanagan said something to the effect that he had been doing that all season and it hadn't come to much. Hales and Flanagan swore at each other. Then they started fighting. Referee Brian Martin had no option but to send off both players.

Everyone was stunned. It was outside most people's experience. There had been a similar incident in Scotland, when two Stranraer players came to blows in 1975, but they had escaped with cautions and very few heard about it. Now

176

Charlton had to complete the game with nine men. They held on and won a replay.

The following week over 10,000 spectators attended the replay in the hope of seeing an upset. The Southern League Premier Division team, unbeaten in 14 games, now had ground advantage, and Second Division Charlton would be without Hales and Flanagan, suspended after their sending-off incident. What they saw was a match which was definitely a bit strange.

Goals by David Campbell and Martyn Robinson gave Charlton a healthy 2–0 lead. Glen Coupland pulled one back with four minutes to play. Then the floodlights went out.

The lights had overheated. There was a 17-minute time-out before they were restored and play resumed. The final two or three minutes were played out with no more score. Maidstone, who had beaten Exeter City in the previous round, were knocked out of the FA Cup for that season. Charlton went out at Bristol Rovers in the fourth round, the only game Mike Flanagan played during the last four months of the season.

Hales and Flanagan both received punishments from Charlton, and Flanagan was later suspended by the club when he implied that the personal difficulties with Hales would prevent him playing. Six months later, after much inactivity, Flanagan moved to Crystal Palace. From there he moved to Queen's Park Rangers. In January 1984, however, Flanagan signed once more for Charlton Athletic, where, for nearly a year he resumed his successful striking partnership with Derek Hales.

THE FALKLAND ISLANDS GAMES

SOUTH GEORGIA, THROUGH THE 1970s

Sometimes the setting is enough to provide a strange game. In 1920–1, at Fishguard on the Welsh coast, players had to swim out to sea to rescue a football before a game could continue. Other games are played next to rivers, with trees overhanging the pitch or with quarries behind one goal. All seem odd when encountered for the first time.

In the 1970s, the British Antarctic Survey team regularly played soccer matches against the crews of ships using the water facilities of the whaling station on South Georgia in the Falkland Isles. Their team was selected from about 20 men on base. They changed in an old cinema and drove to the whaling-station pitch in a tractor and trailer. The pitch, like all unusual settings, was worth a start in goals to the home team. It was cut into the base of a mountain, and local grass covered the stone surface, which, obviously, wasn't the best surface for sliding tackles or the longevity of football boots and footballs. There were no pitch markings but natural boundaries. Three sides were marked by obvious banks. The fourth fell away so that the ball could roll into a stream, a dyke or down drainage holes. Mount Hodges (2,000 ft) acted as a huge spion kop.

A LEGAL PRECEDENT

LEAMINGTON SPA, JANUARY 1980

A foul tackle by Gurdever Basi of Khalsa Football Club broke the right leg of James Condon of Whittle Wanderers in a local league game. Condon was off work for nine months. More than a year after the game he issued a writ suing Basi for damages. He alleged negligence and deliberate and wrongful assault. He won his case.

The case was heard by Judge Wootton at Warwick County Court in March 1984. Basi was found guilty of negligence and Condon was awarded damages of £4,900 plus interest and costs. Basi's appeal was dismissed by Judge Donaldson in May 1985.

For a description of the incident we can rely on the referee's report of the Whittle Wanderers–Khalsa game. An experienced Class 1 official, he wrote this: 'After 62 minutes of play of the above game, a player from Whittle Wanderers received possession of the ball some 15 yards inside Khalsa Football Club's half of the field of play. This Whittle Wanderers' player upon realizing that he was about to be challenged for the ball by an opponent pushed the ball away. As he did so, the opponent (the defendant) challenged, by sliding in from a distance of three or four yards. The slide tackle came late, and was made in a reckless and dangerous manner, by lunging with his boot studs showing about a foot to 18 inches from the ground. The result of this tackle was that (the plaintiff) sustained a broken right leg. In my opinion, the tackle constituted serious foul play and I sent (the defendant) from the field of play.'

Such cases depend on determining what is meant by 'care'. Footballers have a duty to take all reasonable care, bearing in mind the circumstances in which they are placed. In this case Basi was guilty of serious and dangerous foul play which showed a reckless disregard of the plaintiff's safety and fell far below standards which might reasonably be expected in anyone pursuing the game.

So, if you are a player, take care.

THE 'ESCAPE TO VICTORY' GAME

HUNGARY, JUNE–AUGUST 1980

John Huston's remake of the Hungarian film *The Last Goal*, released as *Escape to Victory* in Britain and *Victory* in the United States, was not well received by the critics. The film was more memorable for its soccer sequence than for its portrayal of the realism of war. (If only one could say that about all soccer games.)

Huston's film was set in World War Two. The match revolves around the idea that nations can settle their differences on the soccer field. A German commandant challenges a team of prisoners to a game against their German guards. Captain Colby, played by Michael Caine, organizes the prisoner-of-war team, which contains some very familiar faces. The actors are experienced professional footballers, like Brazilian Pele, Argentinian Ossie Ardiles, former England captain Bobby Moore and Scotland international John Wark. The team's goalkeeper, played by Sylvester Stallone, is more obviously a novice. During filming Stallone discovered that soccer was a very tough sport. Flinging himself around like an acrobat, Stallone broke a finger, damaged his knees and bruised other fingers. When he returned to the United States he described himself as a walking blood clot.

And so, to the climax of the film – the soccer game.

The Germans, to ensure a propaganda victory, have engaged the services of a supportive referee. At half-time the Germans have a 2–0 lead. Then comes a difficult decision for the prisoners. A tunnel has been dug to take them from their dressing-room to safety, but they also want to stay and see through the game – they feel they can win.

Sure enough, they continue the game rather than escape. They pull back the two goals and Stallone saves a penalty. The crowd invades the pitch and the team escape in the confusion.

Escape to Victory was not the first soccer film. The earliest talking picture to include soccer scenes was probably *The Great Game*, which staged a game at Barnes and included in its cast Jack Cock, an England international who was playing for Millwall at the time (1930). Later in the 1930s, the *Arsenal Stadium Mystery* was filmed from Leonard Gribble's book, and a few soccer sequences were set up to portray the fictitious crack amateur team called the Trojans. More recently, Sweden has produced *Stubby*, the United States has given the world *Boys in Company C* and *The Longest Yard*, while Britain chipped in with *Yesterday's Hero* and *Gregory's Girl*, the latter almost certainly being the pick of the lot.

Escape to Victory shows how a soccer game can be staged and filmed to suit an audience's fantasy or the director's concept of an unlikely encounter. There is, however, an element of truth in it. Soccer was indeed played in certain prison camps.

BEHIND CLOSED DOORS

WEST HAM, OCTOBER 1980

The sound of boot on ball echoed around the ground, and the only other noise came from players shouting for the ball and club officials yelling from the sidelines. Such a scene is very familiar in amateur soccer, but this was a vital European Cup-winners Cup-tie between West Ham United and Castilla of Spain. Five hundred police ringed Upton Park to ensure that the game was played behind closed doors. This was West Ham's punishment following crowd trouble during the first leg of the first-round Cup-tie in Spain.

West Ham lost the first leg 3–1 despite leading through David Cross's goal at half-time. Second-half problems included not only the faulty back-passes by Bonds and Pike which led to Castilla goals but also the need for the Spanish police to intervene on the terraces. Fifty West Ham supporters were ejected from the Spanish stadium and one was killed by a bus after the game.

Initially, West Ham were fined £7,750 and ordered to play their next two home European matches at least 300 kilometres from London. Some were arguing that this was a fairly lenient sentence – Rangers, Leeds United and Manchester United had all received European bans after crowd trouble abroad – but when West Ham appealed and presented evidence of the precautions taken, the fine was quashed and the ban on 'away' home matches lifted. Sunderland's offer of a

183

ground wouldn't be needed; West Ham were told to play behind closed doors.

Each club was allowed a 70-man delegation (including players). There were journalists present, and 16 ball-boys were recruited to retrieve the ball from the empty terraces. An attendance of 262 was recorded. Receipts were nil.

For once, the shouts from West Ham officials on the bench – John Lyall, Mick McGiven and Eddie Baily – could be heard clearly by the players (and probably by the police outside). The Spanish radio commentator, too, could be heard chattering to the people back home. The shouts of the players were audibly English and Spanish.

West Ham scored three times in the first half. There was no roar from the crowd, no response to indicate a goal to those inside and outside. David Cross found himself looking at the referee to check whether he had really scored.

Castilla scored and took the game to extra-time. In the empty, eerie stadium Cross scored two more and West Ham took control. They had lost revenue but won the match. After 120 minutes play, the fortunate few went out to tell the world what had happened.

THE BROKEN GOALPOST

CHESTER, SEPTEMBER 1981

Plymouth Argyle's David Kemp headed the ball towards goal. Chester goalkeeper Grenville Millington stretched to make the save. He knocked the ball away and collided with an upright. The goalpost snapped near its base, the crossbar swung freely and the net caved in. Kemp thought he'd scored. Millington was too dazed to know.

That broken goalpost caused the first leg of the Chester–Plymouth first-round League Cup tie to be abandoned after 78 minutes. It became one of the few two-legged Cup ties to need a replay after the *first* leg. The score at the time was 2–2, Kemp having started the scoring, Steve Ludlam managing two for Chester and John Sims squaring the scores just a few minutes before the goal collapsed.

The teams met again at Chester the following week. The replay had one goal each in the first half, and they each had a goal to defend through the whole game . . . rather than just for 78 minutes. Another 1,700 spectators turned out (or was it the same 1,700 as the previous week?) but Chester had to fork out for a new goal and Plymouth bore the costs of another round-trip journey of over 500 miles.

A broken goal doesn't necessarily mean the end of a game. It depends how easily the damage can be repaired. There was a seven-minute delay at Wolverhampton in January 1957 and a 45-minute delay at Lincoln in August 1970. I'm not sure what that says about modern technology. At Lincoln they must have been tempted to muddle through as there were only a couple of minutes to play. Okay, lads, who's going to take off his shirt?

The 1957 incident at Wolverhampton is interesting for another reason. The opponents were Third Division Bournemouth, whose outside-left, Reg Cutler, ran into the netting, broke a goalpost, felt the net come down on top of him and lay tangled up like a caught fish. Cutler later scored the only goal of that fourth round FA Cup tie to provide one of the shocks of the 1950s.

It takes two goals to make a game, and broken goalposts can strike the biggest of clubs. In 1971, Borussia Moechengladbach, leading the West German Bundesliga, were playing at home to Werder Bremen. The score was 1–1 when the game was abandoned two minutes from time after a goal apparatus had collapsed. Borussia lost the game by default, as they were held responsible for not having a replacement goal, but they won the league anyway.

SETTLED OUT OF COURT

DUNFERMLINE, OCTOBER 1981

St Johnstone won 2–1 at Dunfermline in a Scottish League First Division game but there was a matter left outstanding. It was resolved over two years later.

Jim Brown, Dunfermline's captain, had played the ball away when he was struck by John Pelosi's late leaping tackle. Pelosi's feet struck Brown at the front of the knee joint. Ligaments, tendons and muscles were severed below the knee. Despite two operations, it was the end of Brown's career, and he was forced to give up badminton and squash. Two years later the knee still gave him pain.

Pelosi, sent off for the tackle, was fined five weeks' wages and suspended for five weeks by St Johnstone. While away from the club he received a six-month suspension from the Scottish Football Association. Already that season Pelosi had been suspended for five matches after another sending-off incident.

Dunfermline Athletic could not raise a civil action on Jim Brown's behalf. Only he could do it, so Brown sued Pelosi as an individual and St Johnstone as an employer. Two sides of solicitors produced two interpretations of what was meant by 'reasonable care'. Brown claimed care should be in accordance with the accepted rules and conventions of football, that a player should keep control of his feet so as not to endanger other players, and, above all, avoid striking a player on the leg with both feet at the same time.

Pelosi and St Johnstone claimed that the tackle could not be stopped. Also, they claimed that Brown, as a player, had freely and voluntarily agreed to accept the risk of injury in the normal course of the game.

The case did not reach court. St Johnstone made a settlement, believed to be around £20,000, and the rest of Scotland's professional clubs had a close look at their insurance policies.

TEAM ON STRIKE

MAIDSTONE, JANUARY 1983

On New Year's Day, Weymouth were scheduled to play an Alliance Premier League game at Maidstone. Weymouth players were on a high, having won their last nine games, but the club was on a low, pondering an overdraft of £50,000 and losing £700 a week.

Ten players in the squad were based around Bournemouth, 35 miles from Weymouth. These players travelled to games and training by car. They were costing the club over £200 in expenses, and the club had another idea.

Weymouth directors calculated that hiring a mini-bus for Bournemouth-based players would help save £100 a week, but the players thought such a mid-season change would be in breach of their contracts. They sought advice from the Professional Footballers' Association and decided to strike.

On the morning of the Maidstone game the Weymouth team coach set off at 8.30 am. The driver was expecting to pick up the bulk of the squad at Ferndown, a few miles north of Bournemouth, a convenient meeting-place close to the main route east. Weymouth manager Stuart Morgan, Alliance Premier League manager of the month for December, was there. His Bournemouth-based players weren't. The coach had to turn round, and the game was postponed.

The strike lasted 48 hours. For a time it threatened the Monday home game with Bath City, Weymouth's tenth

189

successive victory, and their third round FA Cup tie at Cambridge United, which resulted in a narrow 1–0 defeat.

The club reached a settlement by shelving the mini-bus idea and agreeing to go to arbitration. The Football Association mediated with an increase of £15 in Bournemouth-based players' weekly wages, in lieu of travel expenses. Almost all the players accepted this. The club had to face the consequences of failing to fulfil a fixture.

The Alliance Premier League fined Weymouth £100, ordered them to pay £895 to Maidstone for match expenses and losses and a further £182 towards the costs of the hearing. More controversially, Weymouth were docked 10 league points, taking them out of the Championship race.

By March, when Weymouth's appeal was heard by the Football Association, the Dorset club's season was heading downhill. They had won only one of their last six games, they had to face the possible loss of 10 league points and, at one away game, thieves had broken into their dressing-room during the game. A two-hour hearing at Lancaster Gate cleared the club of a charge of bringing the game into disrepute, ordered the fines and costs to stand, but, justifiably, agreed that the club should lose no league points. The FA offered the chance for three extra points, saying the match with Maidstone should be rearranged.

Maidstone won the game 3–0 but missed the Alliance Premier League Championship by a point. Weymouth ended their crazy season in seventh position.

THE MISSING 78 SECONDS

DERBY, MAY 1983

It was a troubled season for Derby County – only two wins in their first 22 League games and some major spots of bother, particularly in January, when games with Leeds United and Chelsea triggered serious crowd disturbances on successive Saturdays. By the last Saturday of the season, however, the club had rallied. A run of 15 unbeaten League games had pulled them on to the fringe of the relegation zone in Division Two. A win in the last game of the season, at home to Fulham, would ensure safety.

Fulham had their own interests. Malcolm Macdonald's young team had been in the top three for most of the season. A recent bad run had created anxiety, but a win at Derby would guarantee promotion to Division One at Leicester City's expense.

After 75 minutes' play Derby County's Bobby Davison volleyed the first goal of the game. A small pitch invasion by celebrating fans was soon cleared, but the crowd gathered around the edge of pitch, about five or six deep. The pitch became smaller.

Robert Wilson, a Fulham midfield player, was kicked by a spectator while the ball was in play. The touchlines were no longer visible. The referee, Ray Chadwick from Darwen, did his best under the circumstances. Then, when he blew his whistle for offside, the fans, thinking the game was over, swarmed on to the pitch to celebrate Derby's 1–0 win.

Referee Chadwick's watch showed 78 seconds still to play, but the teams had to leave the field. A second Fulham player, Jeff Hopkins, was assaulted in the process. He was too shocked to continue. The referee did not take the players back on to the pitch.

Fulham manager Malcolm Macdonald felt his team deserved a replay. He argued that it wasn't Fulham's fault that the crowd had invaded, cut the game by 78 seconds and interfered with some of the later minutes. Others felt that Derby had deserved to win, looked well on top and the chances of Fulham scoring two goals in the last 78 seconds were minimal. One national newspaper asked readers to recall all those games where away teams had scored two in the last 78 seconds after being one down.

The Football League ruled that the result should stand. Fulham appealed to the Football Association, but with no joy. The only tangible outcome was that Derby County were forced to spend money to improve the security of their ground. They erected perimeter fencing, which stayed a permanent fixture for almost six years.

STRANGE SUBSTITUTION

CAMBRIDGE, FEBRUARY 1984

There have been plenty of strange incidents involving substitutes. Sometimes a newcomer can immediately change the course of a game with a goal. Brendan O'Callaghan of Stoke City scored within ten seconds of coming on as a substitute for his debut (in 1979) and Joe Craig scored with his first touch in a Scottish international shirt (in 1977). On the debit side, at least two players, John Ritchie of Stoke (in 1972) and Bobby Houston of Kilmarnock (in 1979), have been sent off without touching the ball after coming on as substitutes, while John McAlle of Wolves broke a leg almost immediately after taking the field in a 1980 game.

The idea of substituting players during a game met ardent opposition in Britain before the authorities agreed in 1965 (in England) and 1966 (in Scotland). Once the notion of substituting solely for injured players was deemed unworkable, managers were left to contemplate all sorts of tactical options. My favourite is the one used by Cambridge City manager Bill Leivers during a game against Ashford in February 1984.

Leivers, a former Chesterfield and Manchester City fullback, had achieved success as Cambridge United manager, taking them from the Southern League to Division Three, before moving to Cambridge's other club via Chelmsford. He had also had spells as Doncaster Rovers player-manager and

193

Workington Town manager, and was not afraid to experiment.

On 4 February, Cambridge City were 4–0 down to Ashford after 25 minutes play. It was the second successive home game in which City had conceded four in the first half-hour, and, as they had lost the previous one 4–1, Leivers thought it was time to try something different . . . very different. He substituted goalkeeper Nigel Ashman, switched midfield player Trevor Williams into goal, pushed central defender Geoff Hancocks up to centre-forward and dropped Phil Ashworth back from the forward-line to midfield. That left room for the substitute, a natural central defender.

Leivers felt he had to try something drastic to stop Ashford scoring 20 goals, although 19-year-old Ashman wasn't totally to blame for the poor start to the game.

The second half certainly brought the drastic change Leivers was looking for. Ashworth pulled one back, Hancocks got another, Gary French scored a third. That meant seven goals in the net at one end, none in the other. Cambridge City came back from 4–0 down but lost 4–3.

A word of caution, though. Before I hear people suggesting substituting the Manchester United goalkeeper, putting Bryan Robson in goal, Steve Bruce up front and McClair in midfield, I suspect the Leivers plan may not always work so well. It needs a brave manager to try it.

THE 68-HOUR GAME

FLORIDA, AUGUST-SEPTEMBER 1984

When Ernie Schultz, a Miami student, left the field with exhaustion at 9.20 pm on 2 September 1984 it was hardly surprising. At that point the game between North Palm Beach Golden Bears and Palm Beach Piranhas had been going for 51½ hours.

The game eventually lasted 68 hours and 11 minutes, thus breaking the record for the longest-ever game. During this time one player broke an arm and there were several cases of exhaustion, Schultz being the first. The game was finally stopped when one team was down to only six fit players. The teams were following international rules whereby they couldn't continue with less than six on one side.

The game, which started on 31 August, was a systematic attempt at a world record for long play. The previous record (65 hours 1 minute) had been set by the Callinafercy club in Ireland four years previously. In the Florida game, the players averaged 19 years of age. They took five-minute breaks every hour and changed uniform 22 times.

There was a problem at the start. Someone forgot to tell the local police, and when local residents complained of the noise the game was ordered to another field six miles away.

195

'WE WANT TWENTY'

STIRLING, DECEMBER 1984

Stirling Albion had some trepidation about their first round Scottish Cup tie at home to Selkirk. The previous season Stirling were sitting on a huge lead at the top of the Scottish Second Division when they lost 2–1 at home to Inverness Caledonian of the Highland League, the winning goal coming in the last minute of extra-time. Stirling's season had gone downhill from there. They missed the chance of a Cup tie at home to Rangers, and they missed out on promotion. Stirling were still in the Second Division when they were drawn against Selkirk of the Border Amateur League 'B' Division. The prevailing opinion, supported by Stirling manager Alex Smith, was that the game shouldn't be taken lightly. It wouldn't be easy.

Stirling sent chief scout George Rankin to watch Selkirk. He saw them take a 3–0 lead at Leithen Rovers and left before the finish. He didn't see them concede five in the last 20 minutes and go down to a 5–3 defeat.

Stirling Albion, meanwhile, were scoring four in the last 15 minutes of their match at Albion Rovers. Both sides, unwittingly, were warming up for their next week's Cup match, which would establish a British record for this century.

From the start to the end of the game, Stirling Albion showed no signs of underestimating their amateur opponents. Their five first-half goals were all scored by different players

– Irvine (6 mins), Maxwell (12), Ormond (26), Thompson (34) and Dawson (36) – and Walker became the sixth Stirling player on the score-sheet shortly after half-time. Thereafter it was one long procession towards the Selkirk goal.

On another day, Selkirk goalkeeper Richard 'Midge' Taylor might have saved the 13th goal, and there was a suspicion of offside about the 19th, scored by Neil Watt. Otherwise, Stirling were pretty good value for their 20–0 win, and Taylor made some good saves to restrict the score to a score.

Stirling's second-half goalscoring was dominated by David Thompson, a £10,000 signing from Stenhousemuir, who scored six in the second half. The 20 goals were shared by eight players – David Thompson (7), Willie Irvine (5), Keith Walker (2), substitute Neil Watt (2), Scott Maxwell (1), Jimmy Ormond (1), Rab Dawson (1) and Gerry McTeague (1).

Selkirk player-manager Jackson Cockburn had the idea that his team might just be able to frustrate Stirling and catch them in the second half. There's no telling what would have happened had one of Selkirk's two shots gone in, or their one corner-kick had come to something. Towards the end, though, the dreams had been obliterated. I am reminded of a line in a report of Arbroath's 36–0 win over Bon Accord in 1885: 'After the 20th goal, Bon Accord played like a team with no hope.'

There was a touching moment near the end, when Stirling's score was in the high teens. Selkirk officials on the touch-lines collected as many numbers as they could and held them up to indicate they wanted to substitute them all. It was a pity there weren't more than a few hundred spectators present to laugh at the joke.

Stirling supporters, having chanted 'we want ten' after an hour's play, were able to chant 'we want twenty' in the last few minutes. At the end manager Smith thought his team had scored 19 rather than 20 goals. It was an excusable mistake. It was very easy to miss a goal.

This was Stirling Albion's second record of the 1980s. The other was not so positive. They failed to score a goal in the

197

last 13 Scottish League games of 1980–1, altogether playing 1,293 minutes between McPhee's goal (31 January 1981) and Torrance's goal on the opening day of the next season (29 August 1981). That was probably the point at which they started saving them up for poor Selkirk.

Stirling Albion could justifiably be proud of their achievement of recording the biggest victory in British soccer this century, but Selkirk, completely outclassed on the day, could also be proud. Theirs had been an incredible achievement to reach the first round of the Scottish Cup for the first time.

BEER BUT NO SKITTLES

DERBY AND COVENTRY, JANUARY 1985

Burton Albion, a Northern Premier League club from the beer-brewing centre of Britain, were sponsored by a brewery, Ind Coope. Leicester City, their FA Cup third-round opponents, were also sponsored by a brewery, coincidentally Ind Coope. Burton opted to play the tie at the Baseball Ground, home of Derby County, a club sponsored by a brewery, Bass.

There were a few beer cans around the Baseball Ground on the Saturday of the Burton–Leicester game. One landed on the pitch, as did a few coins, and the biggest impact on the game was made by a missile, probably a piece of wood from one of the seats in the stand or possibly a can. Burton goalkeeper Paul Evans didn't see what hit him on the back of the head.

The atmosphere that day was rowdy. Spectators in the stand had difficulty concentrating on the game. Some left before half-time. 'Any Derby County supporters you stand by,' led one chant. 'Cos after the match you're gonna die.'

Leicester scored, Burton Albion equalized. The scores were still level when the critical incident occurred. Paul Evans was hit and needed treatment. The goalkeeper carried on.

At half-time, when the players were given an extra five minutes, Evans was advised by a doctor not to continue. He refused to listen. Burton conceded five more goals, including

199

three in the last 15 minutes. Had Evans been completely fit, it is doubtful he would have saved any of the goals, but people speculated.

Burton Albion directors lodged a formal protest to the Football Association about the 6–1 score. They claimed that Leicester City supporters were responsible for missile-throwing and creating an intimidating atmosphere. The FA met the Friday after the Cup-tie and upheld the protest. They had already created a precedent by ordering a replay of a Cup-tie disrupted by the crowd – Newcastle United against Nottingham Forest in 1974. The draw for the fourth round was again incorrect. Instead of 'Leicester against Carlisle' it should have read 'Burton or Leicester against Carlisle'.

The FA issued another stipulation. The game must be played behind closed doors. After a few problems with the weather, and the need to find a new ground because Derby had a home game, the Burton–Leicester replay was sent to Coventry. Instead of a large boisterous crowd there were snowy terraces and scattered ball-boys. Paul Ramsey scored for Leicester in the fourth minute but Burton raised their game. In the quiet of Highfield Road, the non-Leaguers were unfortunate to lose 1–0 to a team containing a few household names like Gary Lineker, Alan Smith and Ian Wilson.

A POOCH OF A GOAL

STOKE-ON-TRENT, NOVEMBER 1985

To say a dog scored a goal is understating the case. It's almost like saying England scored a fourth in the 1966 World Cup Final when a forward tapped in a pass from a defender. So let's give the dog full credit. This was no everyday goal by a dog. This was supreme opportunism at its best.

David Hall, secretary of Knave of Clubs, recalls the most amazing thing he has ever seen on a football field: 'We were playing Newcastle Town in the Staffordshire Sunday Cup, and I think we were losing 2–0 at the time. One of our players was running down the field with only the goalkeeper to beat. He tried a shot from 15 yards out and miscued it, so it was going well wide. The dog ran on to the field, jumped up at the ball and headed it. The ball flew into the net.'

The dog, a mongrel, disappeared before either secretary had a chance to sign him. He left behind an argument which will continue for years. Should the referee give a goal? David Hall explains; 'There was quite a crowd at Monks Neil Park. Most were laughing at it, but a lot didn't know what the rules would say. The Newcastle players argued that the referee couldn't allow a goal, but the referee did. Our side rejoiced, but their players weren't too happy.'

Newcastle Town hung on to win the Cup tie 3–2.

Like star midfield players, dogs can arrive from nowhere and make an impact on games. They are usually good at keeping their eyes on the ball and dribbling it, but not many are as good in the air as the mongrel at Monks Neil Park. Unfortunately, for at least one footballer, dogs can also be strong tacklers. Chic Brodie was keeping goal for Brentford against Colchester in 1970 when a ferocious white mutt ran full pelt into him just as he was collecting a back-pass. The dog hit Brodie's left knee as he twisted and the goalkeeper suffered serious knee-ligament damage, enough to finish his career at Football League level. The nearest the goalkeepers' union came to exacting retribution on wildlife, as far as I'm aware, was a game in Holland. A high kick from the Feyenoord goalkeeper hit a pigeon which fell dead on to the field.

FIVE PENALTIES IN A GAME

LONDON, MARCH 1989

Referee Kelvin Morton, an accountant from Bury St Edmunds, helped create a new British record when he awarded five penalties in a Division Two game between Crystal Palace and Brighton and Hove Albion. All five came in a 27-minute period either side of half-time.

It was an extraordinary game. Palace's first goal, in the 23rd minute, was sparkling, Ian Wright hitting a volley some considerable distance from goal. When Brighton were reduced to ten men five minutes later – Mike Trusson was sent off for a foul on Eddie McGoldrick – Palace took complete control and earned three penalties in the space of five minutes just before half-time.

Mark Bright had taken over from Neil Redfearn as the Palace penalty-taker, and, in the last home match, he had scored with his first attempt. Bright's method used more power than subtlety. Against Brighton goalkeeper John Keeley he slammed in the first penalty to make the score 2–0, mishit the second penalty against Keeley's legs and opted not to take the third. Ian Wright obliged instead and hit the ball against a post.

Six minutes after half-time Brighton themselves were granted a penalty – Alan Curbishley scored. Then Palace were awarded their fourth of the game. There was no shortage of willing takers. John Pemberton had a try. His shot went over the crossbar.

Brighton were considerably heartened by all this. Palace, on the other hand, having missed three penalties, still only 2–1 ahead, playing against ten men, worrying about their attempts to reach a Second Division play-off position, were growing agitated and nervous. A few more penalty misses might have inspired Brighton defenders to appeal for them in their own area while Palace players shouted 'Never, ref'. Brighton took advantage of Palace's loss of composure to make some late attacks, but Perry Suckling produced a couple of excellent saves and Crystal Palace hung on to win 2–1 when they should have won far more convincingly.

Prior to this Palace–Brighton game, there had been at least five games with four penalty-kicks – St Mirren–Rangers (1904), Burnley–Grimsby (1909), Crewe–Bradford (1924), Northampton–Hartlepool (1976) and Bristol City–Wolves (1977). In addition, other games with a concentration of penalties have certainly occurred outside Britain, including the Argentina–Mexico World Cup game in 1930 when five penalties (some disputed) were awarded. The Palace–Brighton game, on the other hand, aroused no real complaints about the referee's decisions. Palace manager Steve Coppell had only one misgiving – he felt his team should have scored with all four kicks rather than one. As a warning to them not to lose their composure again, he invited them back for extra training the day after the game.

A FLARE-UP FOR FIFA

RIO DE JANEIRO, SEPTEMBER 1989

The FIFA general secretary called it 'the biggest attempt at swindle in the history of FIFA'. It happened midway through the second half of a World Cup qualifying game between Brazil and Chile. Brazil led 1–0 at the time, and looked certain to qualify for the 1990 World Cup Finals. A draw was all Brazil needed, whereas Chile had to win.

Brazil had dominated the game to that point. Careca's goal, on the hour, was small reward for all the Brazilian pressure, but good goalkeeping by Roberto Rojas, the Chilean captain, had kept the lead to one. Rojas was also the principal actor in the drama which followed an incident in the 69th minute.

A 24-year-old Brazilian woman spectator threw a green signal-flare into the Chilean goalmouth while play was at the other end. It floated down, and a cloud of smoke appeared near the goalkeeper Rojas, who fell to the ground holding his face. Chilean players and medical officials gathered round the fallen goalkeeper, and, rather than wait for an official stretcher, they clumsily carried Rojas off the field. The goalkeeper appeared to be bleeding heavily from a cut on the face.

The rest of the Chilean team followed Rojas to the dressing-room. The Brazilian players stood around talking, and match officials waited. When spectators showed signs of impatience, troops were sent to the dressing-room to investigate. FIFA delegates soon joined them. Chile had decided to withdraw from the match, considering lives to be in danger, and the match therefore had to be abandoned. Thousands of the 160,000 spectators waited, many for as long as two hours, in hope that the game would be resumed.

The Chilean team doctor reported that Rojas had required five stitches in a facial cut, but the Brazilians claimed that the blood was simulated. Experts argued that signal-flares were harmless, whereas fireworks might cause such an injury. Photographs showed the flare had not hit Rojas and no blood was initially visible. A FIFA investigation confirmed the deception. Rojas admitted that he had faked his signal-flare injury.

FIFA suspended Rojas from national and international football for life. They also suspended several Chilean officials, including the team doctor, who had issued a false medical certificate, and the equipment official, who had disposed of the goalkeeper's gloves and jersey. Chile were banned from the 1994 World Cup Finals, while Brazilian authorities received a small fine for failing to make adequate security arrangements. Brazil were awarded a 2–0 forfeit victory.

History has shown that a team failing to complete a fixture is likely to be in serious trouble with the football authorities. Later that same month, September 1989, while the Brazil-Chile decision was still being settled, an English non-League team walked off the field. Dunstable Town player-manager Kevin Millett was incensed at a referee who sent off three of his team-mates during an FA Cup tie against Staines Town. He led off the remaining seven, and the tie was abandoned after 38 minutes.

FOOTBALL FOR PIGS

VARIOUS PIG FARMS IN BRITAIN,
FROM JUNE 1990

While the world's football press concentrated on seemingly strange events, like Cameroon's defeat of World Cup holders Argentina, something was stirring at the grassroots of football. More and more pigs were taking up the game.

When Bernard Hoggarth visited the Paris Agricultural Show early in the year, he spotted a Danish product, the Domino Stress Ball, which enabled pigs to play football. Hoggarth bought some balls for his pig business at Cranswick Mill, near Driffield in Yorkshire, and, after successful trials, began marketing Stress Balls in Britain. The manufacturers claim that football-playing pigs are less aggressive and less stressed and therefore happier and more likely to put on weight. You may have heard the same argument applied to human footballers.

The product was publicized around the time of the 1990 World Cup Finals. There were suggestions that an international team of pigs should be managed by Franz Baconbauer, and an English Premier Cut League should include Trotterham Hotspur, Queen's Pork Rangers and Roast Ham United. It would appeal to those football-club groundsmen who claim they've seen dressing-rooms looking like pig-stys.

Pigs are intelligent creatures. When bored, they can

become aggressive, and bite the tails or ears of other pigs in the pen. Hence the need to amuse them. Traditionally, some pig-keepers have suspended chains or left cans in pens to chew on. The Stress Ball is a more sophisticated toy. 'They roll it around the sty, shoot it into corners and leap over it on their way to their fodder,' says the promotion literature. In practice, pigs rely more on dribbling with their snouts than kicking the ball.

Stress Balls are indestructible. They are bright red, about eight or nine inches in diameter and made of sturdy plastic. Each one has a ball-bearing in the middle which rattles as the pigs knock the ball around the pen. A Stress Ball needs to be disinfected and cleaned after each batch of pigs, but can be used time and time again.

On his Yorkshire pig farm, Bernard Hoggarth experimented with one ball in a pen of about 15 pigs. The pigs tended to play with the ball on their own and when one had had enough another took over. No doubt this ability to pass the ball at the right moment can be developed further. Perhaps we will eventually see pigs playing team games, and spectators guaranteed lots of excitement around the pen areas.

It sounds like something out of *Animal Farm*, doesn't it? Those familiar with George Orwell's satirical fairy-tale may recall that the pigs learned to read, lead and stand on hind legs, and Animal Farm became a replica of the human society it had replaced. A manager of a soccer team of pigs would be especially vulnerable to the chop.

Stress Balls have also been supplied to breeding stables for racehorses to play with, but a well-hoofed shot could cause damage if it hits a passing spectator. At the time of going to press, chickens had yet to be approached: the manufacturers were worried about too many fouls.

THE PICK-UP GAME

CAMBRIDGE, EVERY SATURDAY AND TUESDAY

The pick-up game is still alive and kicking. Soccer has not lost its evolutionary charm. Such games do not necessarily take place in streets or back-alleys now, but people still meet informally on some small patch of land, divide into roughly even sides, adapt rules if necessary and do their best to maintain some sort of justice without an official referee.

In the late 1970s and early 1980s I played regularly in a reliable pick-up game started by members of King's College, Cambridge. It was a motley collection of people, men and women, classicists, overseas students, labourers, milkmen, cartoonists and so on. We would meet at some approximate time, decide on the latest fad for picking sides – those in white shirts down that end, size nines against the rest, Britain against the Rest of the World – and start when enough people were ready. Predicting who would arrive late was part of the skill of choosing teams.

There would usually be a debate about rules. In my time we played with small goals – their goal was always smaller than ours – and no players allowed to handle the ball. Goals were allowed only if the ball went along the ground from less than four yards out, although headers and own-goals could be scored from anywhere on the pitch. The size of the pitch varied, depending on how many were playing and whose arguments were accepted.

In the depths of winter, playing with dwindling numbers, more invention was needed. If the numbers were odd we would play around one goal, one team playing into the back of the goal, the other into the front. The goal-line doubled as a halfway-line. The one goalkeeper would be constantly turning around, depending on which team was attacking. This game, of course, can work only if there are no nets.

One day there were seven of us in the snow. There was no obvious four against three team selection, but the Australian among us had a brainwave: we would start with four against three and then anyone scoring a goal would switch to the other side. This seemed very fair in theory. In practice, after ten minutes or so, I found myself 2–0 up and on my own against six of them, wondering who I wanted to score. But it was fun thinking it through, as it is with all novelty matches. Only when a game is established is the participant's choice restricted. Sometimes the discovery of one tactic destroys the fun of invention.

A Second Division team once experimented in training with a two-ball practice-match. The idea was that the players would sharpen up their reactions and vision because twice as much would be happening. Instead, a trio of experienced defenders killed the game when they discovered the tactic of keeping one ball in a boring triangle while their forwards played with the other.

Children, however, retain the spirit of invention. Recently I happened upon four boys playing two-a-side soccer on a disused northern tennis-court. I stopped and watched for almost five minutes as one side attacked ferociously and the other team defended heroically. Then a couple of quick passes and a richochet and the attacking team were through to score. The scorer leapt in the air, twirled his arms, scaled the wire fence and did a lap of honour. Ah, I thought, that's the goal they've been looking for. That's the breakthrough.

That's the goal the commentator's been saying the game needed.

The goalscorer's team-mate took a break from celebrating to announce the score. 'Twenty-seven to us, sixteen to you,' he said.

I walked away, thinking there was still hope for strange soccer matches.